SECOND HOME OWNERSHIP

BANGOR OCCASIONAL PAPERS IN ECONOMICS

General Editor: Jack Revell

> *Professor of Economics,*
> *University College of North Wales,*
> *Bangor.*

NUMBER 6

SECOND HOME OWNERSHIP: A CASE STUDY

Richard de Vane

UNIVERSITY OF WALES PRESS

1975

© UNIVERSITY OF WALES PRESS, 1975

Merthyr House,
James Street,
CARDIFF, CF1 6EU,
United Kingdom.

SBN numbers

The Series: ISBN 0 7083 0448 6
This volume: ISBN 0 7083 0596 2

Printed by photo-litho at the University College of North Wales, Bangor.

EDITOR'S NOTE

The main intention of the series of Bangor Occasional Papers in Economics is to provide a vehicle for the publication of the results of research carried out in the two research institutes at Bangor, the Institute of Economic Research (specializing in regional economics, the economics of tourism and port economics) and the Institute of European Finance. The series also includes adaptations of theses and dissertations by research students in the Department of Economics and contributions by academic colleagues in other universities.

The present volume describes the results of research undertaken by the author while he was employed by the Board of Celtic Studies of the University of Wales. The study was initiated by the Social Sciences Sub-Committee of the Board and carried out under its supervision. Accommodation and other facilities for the research were provided by the Institute of Economic Research.

JACK REVELL

University College of North Wales,
Bangor

Previous volumes in the Series

In preparation

CONTENTS

LIST OF TABLES

LIST OF FIGURES

NOTES AND ABBREVIATIONS

1. Because of rounding, percentages in the tables do not
    necessarily sum to 100, and in those cases where
    absolute numbers are derived from these percentages
    the figures may not sum to 4,386.

2. Symbols   -   nil or negligible
                  ...   not available or not applicable

ACKNOWLEDGEMENTS

I wish to thank the planning and valuation officers at both the County and District levels of local government within Gwynedd for their help and advice and, of course, the second home owners who co-operated in our survey.

My sincere thanks are also due to all members of the Computing Centre of this college, and in particular Dr. P. W. Thomas, for their invaluable help, and to Mrs. Lilian Lund for her great care and patience in preparing the manuscript.

Lastly, I thank our colleagues in the Department of Economics at Bangor for their interest and helpful guidance and, in particular, I should like to mention the constant encouragement and helpful advice of Dr. B. H. Archer, the Director of the Institute of Economic Research, and Professor Jack Revell, our Head of Department.

RICHARD DE VANE

CHAPTER ONE

THE BACKGROUND TO THE STUDY

The nature of the problem

Over the past few years an increasing number of properties have been occupied on a permanent or semi-permanent basis by persons who are normally resident elsewhere. The general increase in mobility and leisure time since the 1930s has put increasing pressure on hitherto remote areas, and with the rising influx of tourists has come an increasing number of persons willing and able to purchase or rent a second property. Over the last decade, this pressure has increased to the extent that real or apparent problems have arisen from the point of view of the 'receiving' regions.

The affected areas tend to manifest some characteristics in common. They are generally areas situated away from major cities or industrial complexes, although the actual distance varies considerably from area to area. Since, in the main, they tend to be peripheral areas, and located near the sea or in upland areas, they are generally areas whose economies are based on agriculture or primary, mainly extractive, industries. In view of economic trends in the 20th century, this implies in the main an ageing, declining population, high unemployment, and an old, usually low quality, housing stock. The disparity in income levels between an exporting area and a receiving area is implicit.

Several factors tend to encourage the potential owner. Housing or site costs are relatively cheap, isolated sites become available when the ageing occupants move into the nearest village or nucleus, traffic densities are low and the person finds the peace and beauty that he seeks. Coupled with this is a possible sense of increased social status, since the second home owner will tend to possess greater mobility, have a higher income and a higher educational level than the receiving population, thus enabling him to see himself as the explorer mingling with, but superior to, the 'locals'.

However, the very factors which would appear to encourage the potential resident are those which cause the problems usually identified with second home ownership, which may give rise to some localized objections to the influx of second home owners. Rural areas are traditionally close communities, and ageing populations are not receptive to change. It is thought that the entrants with higher incomes may be reducing the chances of local young people purchasing a residence. The young people move away and, as the process continues, so the number of young children diminishes until the area can no longer justify the existence of many local services such as village schools, local buses and so on. These services terminate and the remaining young people move to be nearer the new school. Concurrent with this is a reduction in the available active work force,

1

which may either force any local industry to close, or at the very least discourage new industry from entering the area. The process is complete when whole villages, as well as isolated properties, are empty for a large part of the year, and the indigenous population, together with many local services, has gone.

The objections to this process are often localized, since, in the main, community feeling applies only to small geographical areas. The problem becomes particularly acute , however, and the objections become vociferous when this process is seen not only as the destruction of a few isolated communities, but as the submersion of a traditional culture and language.

The need for research

There is an obvious need for research into a problem that arouses strong emotional reactions, which may well be based on erroneous assumptions. Further, certain of the aspects of second home ownership are closely inter-related with local planning decisions.

The social, political and economic aspects of second home ownership may be looked at from three points of view: from that of the owner, from that of the host region concerned, and from that of the nation.

Among the benefits that a second home owner derives from his owner-ship are weekend or vacation residence in an area of his choice, an interest which he may consider as one of his hobbies, namely 'doing up' his property, and the possibility of an income stream and/or a capital gain from his initial expenditure. Among the costs associated with his ownership are rates, rent, standing charges for electricity and water, the maintenance of the second home, the opportunity cost of the money used to purchase the second home, the cost of travelling to service the unit, and so on.

From the standpoint of the host region, second home ownership by persons or other organizations living outside the region may produce benefits and costs of an entirely different order. On the benefit side, there may be such factors as an influx of capital when the property is purchased, followed by a consequent stream of employment-inducing expend-iture on both the property and ancillary services. There may be a general rise in house prices which will increase the capital assets of the indig-enous population, and an increase in the rate income of the local authority. Socially, there may well be a stimulus to local community activity, and a general increase in the awareness of the cultural traditions of the host region. On the cost side there may be, as already mentioned, economic and social costs if second home ownership forces up the price of local properties, thereby encouraging potential property buyers among the local population to leave the region, with all the consequent implications for locally-based industry and service activities. Similarly, if the additional costs of servicing second homes incurred by the local authority is greater than the increase in rate income from second home owners, rates will rise for all property owners, and this will be a direct cost to the region. Regionally, there may be disbenefits through the seasonal influx of second home owners adding to traffic congestion at certain peak periods. These types of social and economic problems may well give rise to political activity aimed against both actual and potential second home owners, particularly in regions which differ significantly in cultural or linguistic traditions, and where the second home owner may be readily identified.

Most of the benefits and costs which have been mentioned above in a regional context apply equally at the national level. The crucial difference here, however, is in terms of the incidence of benefits and costs. The smaller the region, the more valid it becomes to think of the incidence of benefits and costs as being equal to all residents. Conversely, the larger the region under consideration becomes, the less certain can we be that equal incidence will apply, until at the extreme (i.e. national) level, benefits may well accrue to one section of the population, while the costs of second home ownership may fall on an entirely different section. This may be so whether we stratify the population by socio-economic class or whether we divide the area concerned geographically. A strategy for second home ownership which is considered optimal for the nation as a whole may be disastrous for any one particular region or population sector.

In the light of these observations there is a need for research into an activity of which the economic aspects are not well documented. National and regional political decisions, now and in the future, will have economic implications in this field and, in order to facilitate planning, these must be investigated.

This study has been undertaken primarily in order to investigate the extent and nature of second home ownership in Gwynedd, an administrative county in North Wales comprising the old counties of Anglesey, Caernarvonshire and Merioneth. Secondly, we have attempted to measure the economic impact of second home ownership on Gwynedd by examining the expenditure in the area by second home owners and their families.

Definition of second home

Since there is no one readily accepted definition of a second home it was found necessary to derive a suitable definition for this study. The definition used here is as follows:

> *A second home*: any static accommodation unit which may be owned, leased or rented, and which is available for the exclusive use over a twelve-month period of a family unit whose normal daily journey time is minimized at another residence.

This definition may include private houses, flats, chalets, static caravans and houseboats, and will generally exclude hotels, inns, boarding houses and touring caravans. For a detailed exposition of the definition and what it encompasses, the reader is referred to Chapter 6.

The research procedure

Initially we had to establish a definition of a second home which was useful for our study and which might also serve as a basic definition for the comparability of future studies. On achieving this definition, we were then concerned with establishing the number of second homes within Gwynedd. Unfortunately, published data are certainly inadequate, and information derived from local authority sources, whilst useful, only provides a reasonably high percentage of potential second homes. Because these data derived from local authorities, whilst including residences which are *not* second homes, omit a percentage which *are* second homes, we pursued the following course. We investigated all those properties which were potential second homes according to local authority data, including or excluding them as a result of our observations. At the same time we made enquiries in each survey area and, through local knowledge, added to our list of potential second homes. These we surveyed and included or excluded from our total as necessary.

In order to minimize cost, the expenditure survey was undertaken concurrently with this activity. A sample survey of the expenditure by second home owners was undertaken in selected parishes throughout Gwynedd, in order to establish the size and pattern of this expenditure. We required the overall total expenditure figure in order to rank the second home 'industry' compared with other activities in Gwynedd, and the expenditure pattern was used to derive the marginal impact of expenditure by second home owners. This marginal impact was ascertained by running the data obtained in the survey through a computer model of the economy of Gwynedd. The multipliers so derived may be used to compare the relative effect of a change in expenditure in any one industry on output, and also income, within the region.

The survey was conducted by personnel from the University College of North Wales during the 'season' of 1974 on a personal interview basis at the second home. In the event of contact not being established after repeated visits, a prepaid envelope and questionnaire were left at the seasonal home, except in those instances where, through access to local information, it was desirable and possible to write direct to the main home.

CHAPTER TWO

THE EXTENT OF SECOND HOME OWNERSHIP
AND THE CHARACTERISTICS
OF SECOND HOMES IN GWYNEDD

Extent of second home ownership in Gwynedd

The results of our investigation into the extent of second home
ownership in Gwynedd are summarized in Tables 2.1 to 2.6. In these tables
the figures relate to all second homes in Gwynedd, except new developments
and chalets, which were covered in Surveys C and D referred to in Chapter 7.

The first three tables show the structure of housing usage in the
sample parishes by old administrative county. The top half of each table
splits the total housing stock into council houses and private properties.
The bottom half starts off with the number of potential second homes
identified in the manner described briefly in Chapter 1 and detailed in
Chapter 7. Our investigation established that many of these were not
second homes at all, and the table shows the identification of all the
potential second homes, ending with the number of confirmed second homes.
In these tables the categories are defined as follows:

Empty/derelict: houses that have either been empty for many years or those
that are unused because they are derelict.

Permanent homes: houses which are utilized as permanent homes by people
who, for whatever reason, have their rate demand sent to another address.

Retirement homes: those properties which were either (a) originally second
homes but now perform the function of a permanent home or (b) appeared in
the rates book with an out-of-county address for the owner because there
was a time lag involved on moving from the original home to the retirement
home. It does not include second homes to which their owners intend to
retire in the future.

Holiday lets: those properties which are not used as second homes, but
which fulfil the function of providing holiday accommodation for persons
other than the owner on a commercial basis. These may, of course,
subsequently become second homes or, more probably, retirement homes.

Permanent lets: those properties which provide a permanent home for a
family who do not own the property.

Consider first of all Table 2.1 Here the possible second homes,
that is those residences which we identified as in need of investigation,

Table 2.1   The structure of housing use in the sample parishes: Anglesey

Numbers of properties

	Penrhoslligwy	Rhoscolyn	Rhosybol	Llanynghenedl	Llechylched	Llanbadrig	Llaniestyn Rural	Llanddaniel Fab	Total
1. Council houses	8	22	24	154	39	95	-	42	384
2. Private properties	94	205	182	453	224	391	30	229	1,808
3. Total	102	227	206	607	263	486	30	271	2,192
4. Possible second homes	19	82	14	76	56	48	6	41	342
Identified as:									
5. Empty/derelict	1	2	6	8	4	3	1	1	19
6. Permanent homes	1	7	1	17	1	4	1	2	38
7. Retirement homes	-	3	-	-	-	3	-	3	8
8. Holiday lets	4	25	7	44	39	33	5	31	158
9. Permanent lets	1	2	1	-	1	3	1	1	5
10. Others	-	-	-	-	-	1	-	1	
11. For sale	1	-	-	-	-	-	-	-	
12. Confirmed second homes	12	42	8	7	11	31	-	2	106
13. Out-of-county billing addresses	15	66	8	31	18	40	1	8	187

Table 2.2 The structure of housing use in the sample parishes: Caernarvonshire

Numbers of properties

	Henryd	Capel Curig	Maenan	Botwnnog	Llanrhychwyn	Llanbedrog	Aberdaron	Llanaelhaiarn	Total
1. Council houses	24	4	–	38	–	34	10	52	162
2. Private properties	232	113	88	423	91	421	496	463	2,327
3. Total	256	117	88	461	91	455	506	515	2,489
4. Possible second homes	45	40	25	91	33	126	134	69	563
Identified as:									
5. Empty/derelict	1	2	4	6	13	–	3	2	31
6. Permanent homes	1	4	4	10	–	3	11	7	40
7. Retirement homes	–	1	–	3	–	4	4	–	12
8. Holiday lets	–	1	3	1	–	15	1	1	21
9. Permanent lets	37	16	7	48	18	18	54	32	230
10. Others	–	5	–	–	–	1	–	–	5
11. For sale	–	–	–	–	–	1	–	–	1
12. Confirmed second homes	6	12	7	23	2	85	61	27	223
13. Out-of-county billing addresses	8	18	13	46	13	109	81	42	330

Table 2.3   The structure of housing use in the sample parishes: Merioneth

Numbers of properties

	Llanegryn	Llanfair	Talsarnau	Penrhyndeudraeth	Bala	Llangower	Llanymawddwy	Total
1. Council houses	34	25	16	167	368	-	-	610
2. Private properties	122	135	180	565	633	49	80	1,764
3. Total	156	160	196	732	1,001	49	80	2,374
4. Possible second homes	58	24	56	59	61	18	32	308
Identified as:								
5. Empty/derelict	4	2	5	1	1	-	-	13
6. Permanent homes	3	1	6	3	3	1	1	18
7. Retirement homes	1	-	2	-	1	-	-	4
8. Holiday lets	2	1	3	-	-	-	-	6
9. Permanent lets	41	9	13	44	45	6	19	177
10. Others	1	-	-	-	-	-	-	1
11. For sale	-	-	2	1	-	-	-	3
12. Confirmed second homes	7	11	25	10	10	11	12	86
13. Out-of-county billing addresses	17	19	38	42	12	13	17	158

totalled 343.   Of these, some 106 - or just under one-third - were positively identified as second homes.   If we now sum these totals for Tables
2.1 to 2.3 we discover that out of a possible 1,213 second homes 415 were
positively identified as second homes;   this gives an unweighted average
for Gwynedd of 34.0%.

Considering Table 2.2 we see that totals by parish of out-of-county
addresses for rating demands are in row 13.   If we relate these to our
totals by parish of confirmed second homes in row 12, we notice that the
use of rating demands with out-of-county addresses to predict the number of
second homes invariably overestimates, but in no consistent manner.

From Tables 2.1 to 2.3 the other point of major interest is the
high number of permanent lets.   For the parishes concerned these represent
46.3% of possible second homes, and, if we sum these and the council house
totals, we can see that permanent lets in these parishes represent at a
minimum some 9.6% of the total domestic and mixed housing.   The correct
figure is likely to be rather higher because there would be some who did
not pay their own rates and who were not enumerated as part of this study.

Table 2.4   The structure of housing use in the
                   sample parishes: Gwynedd

Numbers of houses

	Anglesey	Caerns.	Merioneth	Gwynedd
1. Council houses	384	162	610	1,156
2. Private properties	1,808	2,327	1,764	5,899
3. Total	2,192	2,489	2,374	7,055
4. Possible second homes	342	563	308	1,213
Identified as:				
5. Empty/derelict	19	32	13	64
6. Permanent homes	38	40	18	96
7. Retirement homes	8	12	4	24
8. Holiday lets	8	21	6	35
9. Permanent lets	158	230	177	565
10. Others	5	5	-	10
11. For sale	-	1	3	4
12. Confirmed second homes	106	223	86	415
13. *Out-of-county billing* *addresses*	187	330	158	675
Confirmed second homes as % of *all houses in sample*	*4.8*	*9.0*	*3.6*	*5.8*
Confirmed second homes as % of *all private houses in sample*	*5.9*	*9.6*	*4.9*	*7.0*
Confirmed second homes as % of *out-of-county billing addresses*	*56.7*	*67.6*	*54.4*	*61.5*

Table 2.4 shows not only the totals of Tables 2.1 to 2.3 but also the percentage density for all houses in the sample. The row showing the percentage density for all private houses in the sample is simply the previous row after abstracting the council housing densities. The final row in Table 2.4 shows second homes as a percentage of out-of-county billing addresses. It is inserted here in view of the use made in some studies of the total out-of-county billing addresses as a proxy for second home numbers.

Tables 2.5 and 2.6 both show the numbers of confirmed second homes in the 23 parishes in our sample, but the four classes are defined in different ways. In Table 2.5 the classes are based on the numbers of potential second homes with which we started our survey, whereas in Table 2.6 the parishes have been reclassified according to the numbers of confirmed second homes. A standard statistical test showed that these results were most unlikely to have been caused by sampling error.

Table 2.5   Sample parishes arranged in expected densities of second homes

Numbers of confirmed second homes

Class A 0.0 - 9.9%		Class B 10.0 - 19.9%		Class C 20.0 - 29.9%		Class D 30.0% & over	
Llaniestyn Rural	–	Llanynghenedl	7	Llechylched	11	Rhoscolyn	42
Rhosybol	1	Penrhoslligwy	12	Aberdaron	61	Llanbedrog	85
Llanddaniel Fab	2	Botwnnog	23	Talsarnau	25	Llangower	11
Llanbadrig	31	Llanrhychwyn	2				
Llanaelhaiarn	27	Llanfair	11				
Capel Curig	12						
Maenan	7						
Henryd	6						
Llanymawddwy	12						
Bala	10						
Penrhyndeudraeth	10						
Llanegryn	7						
Total	125		55		97		138
Percentage of total confirmed second homes	*30.1*		*13.3*		*23.3*		*33.3*

Characteristics of second homes

Here we shall present some descriptive statistics of second homes and their owners, together with some explanation of both our interpretation of second home owners' responses at the interview level and our interpretation of the results. It should be borne in mind at all times that responses to questions are to a certain extent limited by the alternative responses allowed and that, whilst we have in some cases allowed flexibility by including an 'other' category (see, for example, response 2, Questionnaire A1, Appendix II), this was not possible in the majority of cases. Reference should therefore be made to the relevant questionnaire when interpreting the tables.   The sections are those of the questionnaires in Appendix II.

Table 2.6   Sample parishes arranged in derived densities of second homes

Numbers of confirmed second homes

Class A 0.0 - 9.9%		Class B 10.0 - 19.9%		Class C 20.0 - 29.9%		Class D 30.0% & over
Llaniestyn Rural	-	*Capel Curig*	12	*Rhoscolyn*	42	
Rhosybol	1	*Llanymawddwy*	12	*Llanbedrog*	85	
Llanddaniel Fab	2	Penrhoslligwy	12	*Llangower*	11	
Llanbadrig	31	*Aberdaron*	61			
Llanaelhaiarn	27	*Talsarnau*	25			
Maenan	7					
Henryd	6					
Bala	10					
Penrhyndeudraeth	10					
Llanegryn	7					
Botwnnog	23					
Llanrhychwyn	2					
Llanfair	11					
Llechylched	11					
Llanynghenedl	7					
Total	155		122		138	-
Percentage of total confirmed second homes	37.3		29.4		33.3	-

Note: Parishes that have changed class from Table 2.5 are distinguished in italic type.

Section 1: type of property

This question is a fairly straightforward one, with little opportunity for individual interpretation.   The only point of interest in Table 2.7 is that 3.8% of second homes in our sample were flats;   these tended to be luxury flats in very large houses.

Table 2.7   Type of property

	Percentages	Numbers
House	30.0	1,315
Bungalow	23.8	1,043
Cottage	42.5	1,864
Flat	3.8	166
Total	100.0	4,386

Section 2: form of property

Table 2.8 shows that about 72% of second home properties are detached. Since we know that detached cottages and houses are less common in villages than terraced or semi-detached properties, it will be interesting to observe later whether the house and cottage sectors together comprise a high proportion of the 72% and, if so, whether from this we are able to derive a proxy measure of second home ownership.

Table 2.8   Form of property

	Percentages	Numbers
Detached	71.9	3,153
Semi-detached	8.1	355
Terraced	20.0	877
Other	–	–
Total	100.0	4,386

Section 3: age of property

We see from Table 2.9 that the majority of houses purchased by second home owners are 19th century houses, and that houses built during the last ten years are the second largest group. This is probably rather higher than expected, and presumably it refers both to 'new development' houses and other purpose-built second homes, which have mushroomed in selected areas of Gwynedd.

Table 2.9   Age of property

	Percentages	Cumulative percentages	Numbers
0 - 10 years	18.8	18.8	824
11 - 30 years	6.9	25.6	302
31 - 75 years	12.5	38.1	548
Over 75 years	61.9	100.0	2,714
Total	100.0		4,386

Section 4: garden size of property

The interesting point to note in Table 2.10 is that some 9% of second homes do not have a garden, which would tend to imply that they are 'new developments', flats, or situated in villages and towns.

12

Table 2.10   Garden size of property

	Percentages	Cumulative percentages	Numbers
No garden	9.4	9.4	412
Less than 0.25 acre	51.3	60.6	2,250
0.25 - 1 acre	29.4	90.0	1,289
1 - 5 acres	6.9	96.9	302
6 - 10 acres	1.9	98.8	83
Over 10 acres	1.3	100.0	57
Total	100.0		4,386

Section 5: location of property

Table 2.11 should be treated with some caution, since, although a fairly accurate assessment was possible during personal interviews, not every postal response can be deemed an accurate response between the hamlet and village values. Further, a property on the outskirts of a village may only be considered to be part of that village if one pre-supposes a certain level of public or private transport, and in the latter category this in itself tends to presuppose a certain income and age band.

Table 2.11   Location of property

	Percentages	Numbers
Isolated	34.4	1,508
Hamlet	20.6	903
Village	41.9	1,837
Town	3.1	135
Total	100.0	4,386

Section 6: tenure of property

The figures in Table 2.12 are to be expected because a high proportion of second home users will probably come from a property-owning background, and will thus only lease or rent a property in those few pockets where the present owners have no wish to sell. In this way the percentage who are prepared to rent or lease may provide interest to anyone attempting to derive an attraction index; in these pockets the environment presumably outweighs the desire to own, which would manifest itself in a move to another area.

Table 2.12   Tenure of property

	Percentages	Numbers
Owned	95.6	4,193
Leased or rented	4.4	193
	100.0	4,386

Section 7: date of acquisition of property

Since the figures of Table 2.13 are grossed up from a sample, some individual years are missing. However, from the curve derived in Figure 2.1 we can see that the rate of growth of second home ownership was fairly constant between 1918 and 1945. The rate of take-up increased in the few years immediately after the war, perhaps as a result of enforced immobility during the war and retirement arrangements. The rate then levelled off to its pre-war level until the early 1950s, when it began to increase at a fairly rapid rate until the early 1960s, after which the rate of take-up levelled out or perhaps fell slightly. The increase from the early 1950s may well have coincided with the end of petrol rationing and the changing rate of private car ownership, whilst the levelling out in the rate of increase may well be accounted for by the economic instability of the early and middle 1960s. The rate of take-up increased rapidly again during the late 1960s, reaching a peak in 1971, from which it has plummeted to a rate of take-up similar to that of the late 1950s.

Figure 2.1   The rate of second home acquisition

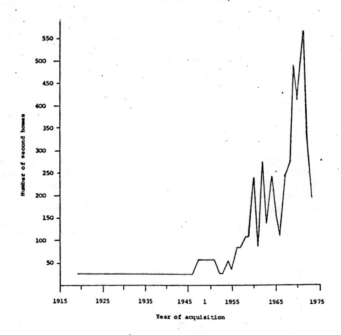

14

Table 2.13   Property acquisition date

	Percentages	Cumulative percentages	Numbers
1919 – 1924	.6	.6	26
1925 – 1931	.6	1.3	26
1932 – 1945	.6	1.9	26
1946	.6	2.5	26
1947 – 1951	1.3	3.8	57
1952	.6	4.4	26
1953	.6	5.0	26
1954	1.3	6.3	57
1955	.6	6.9	26
1956 – 1957	1.9	8.8	83
1958	2.5	11.3	109
1959	2.5	13.8	109
1960	5.6	19.4	245
1961	1.9	21.3	83
1962	6.3	27.5	276
1963	3.1	30.6	135
1964	5.6	36.3	245
1965	3.8	40.0	166
1966	2.5	42.5	109
1967	5.6	48.1	245
1968	6.3	54.4	276
1969	11.3	65.6	495
1970	9.4	75.0	412
1971	13.1	88.1	574
1972	7.5	95.6	328
1973	4.4	100.0	192
Total	100.0		4,386

Section 8: how the property was acquired

The 'not applicable' response in Table 2.14 refers to those persons who rent or lease their properties, and is not a non-response. Of course, looking at the possible answers, it is obvious that they are not mutually exclusive in that, for example, a second home owner might also qualify as a distant owner. However, although the question entered the questionnaire as a means of establishing a talking point with the respondent, it may be reasonable to deduce that some 65% of second home owners had spent suffic- ient time in the area prior to purchasing to establish some relationship with the local population. Since this is almost certainly true for those who lease or rent their second homes, it would appear that, in total, some 70% of second home owners had prior interest in and knowledge of the area.

Table 2.14   How the property was acquired

	Percentages	Numbers
A local owner	45.0	1,973
A second home owner	21.9	960
A distant owner	5.6	245
An estate agent	12.5	548
Purpose built	10.6	464
Not applicable	4.4	192
Total	100.0	4,386

Section 9: was it a cash purchase?

The 'not applicable' response in Table 2.15 comprises those who rent or lease and those who, for one reason or another, acquired their properties free. As such, it does not constitute a non-response. We were very careful to ensure that respondents were aware that a cash purchase excluded not only building society loans but also short-term or long-term bank loans. Thus, even those who purchased their second home with the aid of a six-months' loan would be excluded from the 'cash purchase' result. Therefore purchases seem to be mainly independent of the housing loan market.

Table 2.15   Was it a cash purchase?

	Percentages	Numbers
Cash purchase	81.3	3,837
Not cash purchase	12.5	548
Not applicable	6.2	276
Total	100.0	4,386

Section 10: annual rent

Note that the zero rent payments in Table 2.16 are made by owners of their own second homes. Not surprisingly, annual rent payments tend to be low, since many of the rented properties will be isolated and in poor condition.

16

Table 2.16   Annual rent payments

Rent £	Percentages	Cumulative percentages	Numbers
Zero	95.6	95.6	4,193
1 - 50	2.5	98.1	109
51 - 150	1.3	99.4	57
151 - 300	.6	100.0	26
Total	100.0		4,386

Section 11: bedrooms and bedspaces

The high proportion of two- and three-bedroomed properties in Table 2.17 reflects the high proportion of old rural houses used as second homes. We asked these two questions in order to see whether there was a strong relationship between the number of bedrooms or the number of bedspaces (Table 2.18) and the size of the usual visitor group (see Section 12 below). The mean number of bedrooms was 2.844 with a standard deviation of 1.019, compared with a mean number of bedspaces of 5.444 with a standard deviation of 1.628. This implies an average bedroom occupancy rate of just under two.

Table 2.17   Number of bedrooms

Bedrooms	Percentages	Cumulative percentages	Numbers
1	3.1	3.1	135
2	38.8	41.9	1,701
3	36.9	78.8	1,618
4	15.6	94.4	684
5	4.4	98.8	192
6	.6	99.4	26
8 or more	.6	100.0	26
Total	100.0		4,386

Table 2.18   Number of bedspaces

Bedspaces	Percentages	Cumulative percentages	Numbers
2	2.5	2.5	109
3	4.4	6.9	192
4	30.0	36.9	1,315
5	16.9	53.8	741
6	18.8	72.5	824
7	10.6	72.5	464
8 or more	16.9	100.0	741
Total	100.0		4,386

Section 12: usual visitor group size

The mean visitor group size derived from Table 2.19 was 4.200 with a standard deviation of 1.491. This is consistent with an average bedroom occupancy rate of just under two, since the cumulative frequency for visitor group sizes 4, 5, and 6, namely 64.4%, is reasonably similar to the cumulative frequency of the two- and three-bedroomed properties.

Table 2.19   Visitor group size

Group size	Percentages	Cumulative percentages	Numbers
1	.6	.6	26
2	15.0	15.6	657
3	14.4	30.0	631
4	32.5	62.5	1,425
5	16.9	79.4	741
6	15.0	94.4	657
7	3.1	97.5	135
8 or more	2.5	100.0	109
Total	100.0		4,386

Section 13: state of the property when it was acquired

Two points of interest in Table 2.20 may be noted. The first is that the percentage of new properties purchased appears surprisingly large. This reflects, however, the recent new developments and purpose-built homes in pockets in Gwynedd. Secondly, we were concerned that the large percentage acquiring old properties in need of modernization might well reflect the availability of grant aid on these properties. Thus we looked at the choices people would have made had the final costs been equal (i.e.

cost of purchase plus modernization in the case of the first category) and, secondly, the number of properties which had received grant aid.   It must be emphasized, however, that Sections 13 and 14 may only be taken as an indication, since no attempt was made to define the categories concerned, and the answers to Section 14 are by their very nature subjective.

Table 2.20   Property state when acquired

	Percentages	Numbers
Old property in need of modernization	53.8	2,359
Modernized old property	21.3	934
New property	25.0	1,096
Total	100.0	4,386

Section 14: property preferences of second home owners

Comparing Tables 2.20 and 2.21 we notice that, whereas the percentages of those people preferring a modernized old property or a new property relate quite well with their actual acquisitions, the percentage.

Table 2.21   Property preference

	Percentages	Numbers
Old property in need of modernization	40.0	1,754
Modernized old property	23.1	1,013
New property	23.1	1,013
No preference	13.8	605
Total	100.0	4,386

Note: Respondents were asked to choose between these types of property on the assumption that the final costs of each type were equal.

preferring an old property in need of modernization is lower than actual purchases, and is exactly compensated for by those people showing no preference in the type of property they would purchase.   If this 'no preference' option is made up of people who have purchased old properties in need of modernization, we might well expect that something of the order of 13-14% of second home owners had received grants on their properties.   Before we investigate this we must mention that, in response to the question on property preference, a number of respondents suggested that they disliked the implicit assumption that old properties were necessarily in need of modernization, and that they preferred them 'just old'.   These respondents were placed in the 'in need of modernization' category, but they presumably represent the 'back to nature' type of second home owner.

Section 15: how many second home owners have received grant aid?

From Table 2.22 we find, in fact, that 11.2% of second home owners received a grant on their property, and the mean grant received by those who received grant aid, namely 491 home owners, was £541, totalling £265,631. Thus the mean grant for all second home owners was £60 and, as shown above, 88.8% of second home owners did not receive a grant. We have no details of refused applications, and the policies pursued by some of the old district councils may well have contributed to the low numbers receiving grants. However, bearing in mind the type of housing stock acquired, this figure is surprisingly low but, as far as we are able to judge, accurate. We spent much time during interviews attempting to cross-check this response and were often told that either the time and trouble were not worth the money or that the second home owner did not feel entitled to the grant, which he considered unnecessary.

Table 2.22   Grant aid to second homes

	Percentages	Numbers
No grant aid	*88.8*	3,894
Grant aid	*11.2*	491
Total	*100.0*	4,386

CHAPTER THREE

THE CHARACTERISTICS
OF SECOND HOME OWNERS

In this chapter we shall present some descriptive statistics relating to second home owners. Note once again that the limitations in the interpretation of the data, discussed at the beginning of Chapter 2, apply.

Personal characteristics

Section 1: reasons for acquiring a second home

In Table 3.1 the totals do not equal 100.0 and 4,386 respectively since multiple answers were given by those owners who were unable to identify one single reason. These results must be interpreted carefully, since the answer is, of course, open to bias by the period of time that has

Table 3.1   Acquisition purposes

	Percentages	Numbers
Wish to sub-let	-	-
As a capital investment	4.4	192
For eventual retirement	31.3	1,372
For holiday/weekend accommodation	76.9	3,372
To be near friends/relatives	6.9	302
Other reasons	8.1	355
Total	127.6	5,593

elapsed since the purchase date. Nevertheless, not surprisingly, there is a strong response in terms of holiday/weekend use and retirement. The 'other reason' category represents responses ranging from the 'need for private holiday accommodation due to illness' to 'a strong sense of identity with the Welsh culture and customs'. Our observations on the retirement question are left to a later section.

Section 2: expected year of retirement

We asked this question for two reasons. Certainly we were

interested in the actual expected year of retirement, a knowledge of which may well be important for planning purposes, but secondly - and of interest in this section - because we wished to establish a proxy for the age of the head of the household.   We discovered a mean retirement year of mid-1984/85, with a standard deviation of 13.429 years.   Given that second home owners retire at 65 years of age, this would suggest that the average second home owner is now about 55 years old.   However, our interviewing enabled us to deduce that, whilst there are a few second home owners who will never effectively retire, the majority appeared to consider the age of 58-60 years a reasonable time to retire;   therefore we might well deduce that the average age of the present second home owner is in the 45-55 age bracket.

Section 3: employment tenure of second home owners

Not surprisingly, Table 3.2 shows that none of the second home owners interviewed was unemployed, since presumably in a prolonged period of unemployment it is likely that either the primary or secondary home would be sold, in either case removing the respondent from the category of second home owner.   Equally unsurprising is the high proportion, although not a majority, of second home owners who are self-employed.   Apart from

Table 3.2   Conditions of employment

	Percentages	Numbers
Employed	53.1	2,328
Self-employed	38.8	1,701
Unemployed	-	-
Retired	8.1	355
Total	100.0	4,386

any tax advantages which may accrue to self-employed businessmen, it may be that the small fraction of self-employed businessmen who own second homes have higher than average disposable income.   Further, they are able to allocate their time in such a way as to derive more benefit from second home ownership than the majority of the employed population.   The final point to notice from Table 3.2 is that 8.1% of second home owners are retired.   This point is important in the context of both retirement decisions and income structure of second home owners, and will be referred to later.

Section 4: occupational status of second home owners

From Table 3.3 see see that the total percentage of second home owners who may be thought of as 'blue collar' workers (the first five groups) is 7.6%.   This contrasts unfavourably with the results of the Wye College study previously mentioned, which derived a total in the order of 20%, but the latter figure includes caravans and chalets which are, in the main, excluded from our definition.   Nevertheless, 7.6% is surprisingly high, and tends to be misleading for the following reasons.   The blue collar workers interviewed in our survey tend either to rent their main home or to have purchased jointly their second home with another family or families. Further, the second home owners who fall into the farm category tend to be farm workers living in tied houses, who have bought their second home as a property investment for retirement purposes, as well as for holiday accommodation.   Thus, while this figure is accurate for the Gwynedd population of second home owners, it would be inaccurate to make any predictions about the U.K. as a whole without some knowledge of those blue collar workers who live in rented or tied accommodation.

Table 3.3   Occupation group

	Percentages	Numbers
Factory	1.9	83
Transport	.6	26
Building	-	-
Farm	1.3	57
Other manual	3.8	166
Professional	54.4	2,385
Director, proprietor, manager	30.6	1,342
Shop, personal service	1.3	57
Office and all others	6.1	267
Total	100.0	4,386

Eighty-five per cent of second homes are owned either by professional persons or by directors, proprietors and managers.   It would be unrealistic to consider either category on its own since many of the respondents fell into both categories, and the allocation between these two was often arbitrary.   This high percentage is not surprising for the following reasons:

(a)   We should expect the majority in these categories to have either a high income or convertible assets, or both;   this would enable them to save a higher proportion of their income if they desired, and also it would make it easier for them to raise finance for their purchase.   Since, in the event, we know (from Table 2.15) that 81.3% of second home owners bought their second homes with cash, we may consider that this sort of purchase was facilitated by a fairly wealthy family background.   (This age group now between 45 and 55 would, in the main, have paid for their higher education.)

(b)   Since, as a group, they probably had a higher level of mobility through personal transport before the motor car boom in the late 1950s and early 1960s, they probably have a close contact with the area over many years.

(c)   Whilst the majority of the 85% are accountants or members of the medical profession, a high proportion are teachers and, to a lesser extent, university staff, who tend to have longer vacations than the average person, and who therefore have an incentive to have a permanent holiday base.   These people would have had the time to find and work on second homes and, in the main, purchased their properties very early on.

Section 5: family income of second home owner on purchasing

We asked for family income on our questionnaire since we believed that this was probably more important than merely the income of the head of the household in determining whether a second home could be acquired. We also felt that we were more likely to get a response to this question. Table 3.4 shows gross family income in the year of purchase; since some 60% of second homes were purchased between 1965 and 1974 (see Table 2.13), this probably understates the comparative current income because of subsequent wage and salary increases.

Table 3.4   Family income on acquisition

Income £	Percentages	Cumulative percentages	Numbers
Less than 3,000	36.3	36.3	1,592
3,001 - 3,500	5.0	41.3	219
3,501 - 4,000	7.5	48.8	328
4,001 - 4,500	11.9	60.6	521
4,501 - 5,000	5.6	66.3	245
5,001 - 5,500	3.8	70.0	166
5,501 - 6,000	4.4	74.4	192
6,001 and over	25.6	100.0	1,122
Total	100.0		4,386

From Table 3.4 we can see that approximately 62% of second home owners had family incomes either below £3,000 per annum or above £6,000. The lower income group are probably owners who purchased their second homes earlier on in life, together with a high number of lower paid professional people, e.g. teachers. The higher income group probably consists mainly of businessmen, professional people and managers.

Section 6: family income of second home owner now

Again Table 3.5 shows gross family income. Here we see once more that the two highest relative frequencies are in the lowest and highest

Table 3.5   Family income now

Income £	Percentages	Cumulative percentages	Numbers
Less than 3,000	15.6	15.6	684
3,001 - 3,500	13.8	29.4	605
3,501 - 4,000	8.8	38.1	385
4,001 - 4,500	9.4	47.5	412
4,501 - 5,000	6.3	53.8	276
5,001 - 5,500	4.4	58.1	192
5,501 - 6,000	4.4	62.5	192
6,001 and over	37.5	100.0	1,644
Total	100.0		4,386

24

income bands for the same reasons.   Note also that our income bands stop
at £6,000 per annum.   A very high proportion of second home owners in the
£6,001 and over band appear to earn in excess of £10,000 per annum (i.e.
some 25-30% of all second home owners).

Section 7: education and the second home owner

We asked this question as something of a talking point near the end
of the interview rather than for information.   There is obviously some
overlap between options two and three, in that, for example, chartered
accountants would fulfil both requirements, so the answers must be treated
with caution.

Table 3.6   Termination of full time education

Age	Percentages	Numbers
15 or less	11.3	495
15 - 20	37.5	1,644
After degree or other qualific- ation at university or similar	51.3	2,250
Total	100.0	4,386

In Table 3.6 presumably the 11.3% who finished their full time
education at or below fifteen years of age are in the blue collar workers
and self-made men categories.

Section 8: present location of primary homes by area

The West Midlands provides forty-nine percent of all second home
owners.   Together with the North West, it accounts for some seventy-five
percent of the total.   These owners would tend to live within a 145-mile
radius of their second home, with an off-season journey time of approximately 3 hours, rising to 4½ hours in the tourist season.

Table 3.7   Location of primary homes

Location	Percentages	Numbers
Scotland	2.0	88
North East	4.4	193
North West	25.0	1,096
East Midlands	6.9	303
West Midlands	49.0	2,149
South East	8.7	381
South West	2.0	88
Wales	2.0	88
Total	100.0	4,386

Section 9: retirement and second home owners

Since retirement by second home owners rather than just holiday use represents an important aspect of the use of housing, we investigated this question in some detail.   In answer to our questionnaire we received the answers shown in Table 3.8   Notice that the 'not decided' category constitutes the largest single category and almost 40% of the total.   Those who stated that they would retain the use of their second home and use it for much the same period as they do now constituted some 24% (in future referred to as 'same use').   The only reasonable estimate that we are able to make is that probably some 30% of this group ('not decided') would move into group 5 if it were economically possible.   However, these results are not inconsistent with the answers in Table 3.1:   although 31.3% purchased their properties for eventual retirement and only 26.3% now intend to retire and live permanently at their second home, we should expect (a) some wastage due to external pressures and (b) some reassessment as incomes change.

Table 3.8   Retirement decision of second home owner

	Location	Percentages	Numbers
1.	To second home	26.3	1,153
2.	Within the county	5.6	245
3.	Elsewhere	5.6	245
4.	Not decided	38.8	1,701
5.	Retain use of second home	23.8	1,043
	Total	100.0	4,386

Table 3.9   Retirement decision after apportionment of 'not decided'

	Location	Percentages	Numbers
1.	To second home	42.9	1,883
2.	Within the county	9.1	400
3.	Elsewhere	9.1	400
4.	Not decided	–	–
5.	Same use	38.9	1,704
	Total	100.0	4,386

It would perhaps be reasonable to allocate the 38.8% in group 4 in Table 3.8 between the other groups in the proportion to which the groups constitute the total, giving us then perhaps upper limits on the numbers of second home owners likely to retire part-time or full-time to Gwynedd.   The results of this calculation are shown in Table 3.9.

We then considered the question of the location of property which would be used for retirement purposes.   We relate the retirement decision to whether the property is isolated, in a hamlet, a village or a town.

Table 3.10　　Retirement decision by location of property

Percentages

		Isolated	Hamlet	Village	Town
1.	To second home	23.6	33.3	23.9	40.0
2.	Within county	7.3	3.0	6.0	-
3.	Elsewhere	3.6	-	9.0	20.0
4.	Not decided	38.2	45.5	37.3	20.0
5.	Same use	27.3	18.2	23.9	20.0
	Total	100.0	100.0	100.0	100.0
% of all second homes		*34.4*	*20.6*	*41.9*	*3.1*

Table 3.11　　Retirement decision by location of property

Numbers

		Isolated	Hamlet	Village	Town
1.	To second home	356	301	439	54
2.	Within county	110	27	110	-
3.	Elsewhere	54	-	165	27
4.	Not decided	576	411	684	27
5.	Same use	412	164	439	27
	Total	1,508	903	1,837	135

From Tables 3.8 and 3.11 we can see that 23.6% of those second home owners possessing an isolated second home, in total 356, intend at this time to retire to their property. As we pointed out earlier, the term 'isolated' tends to be a relative term, but perhaps an ageing retired population losing mobility and probably with a lower income would be at risk in these proper- ties. If we include those who intend 'same use' and 'not decided', we have a maximum possible retirement population of 1,344 isolated properties. This, of course, does not mean that these will all be occupied by retired people at one time. If we examine Figure 3.1 we can see that there are two peaks in the retirement pattern but apart from that the movement is fairly gradual, settling at about 70 homes per year. This pattern relates, of course, to all second home owners.

Figure 3.2 shows the retirement pattern of those second home owners who are retiring to their second homes. From this we can see that, whilst the pattern is similar, the rate is very different. Figure 3.3 shows the combined rates of groups one and five (i.e. definite retirement homes plus those homes used for the same number of days by couples who will by then be retired).

Figure 3.1   Retirement of all second home owners by year of retirement

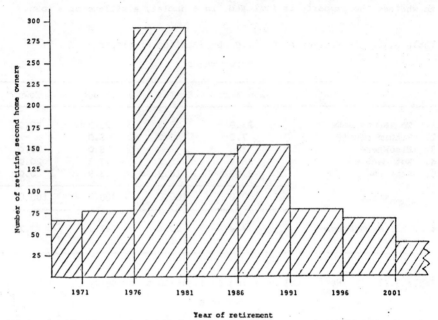

Figure 3.2   Retirement to second home by year of retirement

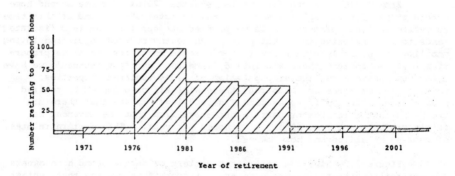

Figure 3.3   Retirement to second home and same use by retirement year

We wondered whether the length of ownership of the property had a
great deal to do with the retirement decision.   We therefore related
acquisition date of those intending to retire to their second home to the
rate of take-up in Figure 3.4   and acquisition date of those undecided to
the rate of take-up in Figure 3.5.   Looking at the two histograms there
appears to be no significant relationship between the period of acquisition
and the retirement decision.

We then looked at the level of education and the retirement decision
(see Table 3.12) to see if it were possible to pick out those second home

Table 3.12   Retirement decision by level of education

Education finished	To second home	Within county	Elsewhere	Not decided	Same use
15 or less	23.8	-	11.1	4.8	10.5
15 - 20	38.1	22.2	55.5	38.7	34.2
After degree, etc.	38.1	77.8	43.4	56.5	55.3
Total	100.0	100.0	100.0	100.0	100.0
% of all second homes	26.3	5.6	5.6	38.8	23.8

owners retiring to their second homes by examining their level of education. No significant relationship was found between these variables.

Finally we examined the relationships between the retirement decision and the level of present family income. Table 3.13 is a cross-tabulation relating location of retirement to present family income. We

Table 3.13 Location of future retirement by family income now

Numbers

Income £	To second home	Within the county	Elsewhere	Not decided	Same use	Total	Percentages
Less than 3,000	215	27	–	138	301	682	15.5
3,001 – 3,500	192	109	–	247	55	603	13.7
3,501 – 4,000	141	–	27	138	83	389	8.9
4,001 – 4,500	138	27	27	192	27	411	9.4
4,501 – 5,000	140	–	27	54	54	275	6.3
5,001 – 5,500	29	–	54	82	27	192	4.4
5,501 – 6,000	55	27	–	82	27	192	4.4
6,001 and over	244	54	109	768	467	1,642	37.4
Total	1,154	244	244	1,701	1,043	4,486	100.0

ran a correlation of the retirement decision on income and discovered no significance in the relationship. In sum, we derived totals of those definitely retiring to their second homes and then attempted to allocate the undecided category in a meaningful way. We examined the relationship of the retirement location decision to the location of the property, the retirement of second home owners over time, and the retirement of second home owners retiring to their second homes, to which we added the retirement rates of those intending 'same use'. We then looked at the acquisition dates of those retiring to their second homes and compared this pattern with that of the undecided group (group 4). We examined the relationship between the retirement decision and the present level of family income.

Occupancy rates of second homes, 1973-74

Below we present tables showing the rate of occupancy of second homes by different types of users. The term 'traditional' used refers to the present second home structure in Gwynedd, which comprises mainly old cottages and houses. Data derived separately for old cottages and houses would be so similar as to present an unnecessary encumbrance. It should also be remembered that chalets, in the main, do not qualify for inclusion as second homes according to our definition, and are included for comparison purposes only.

Figure 3.4   Retirement to second home by acquisition date

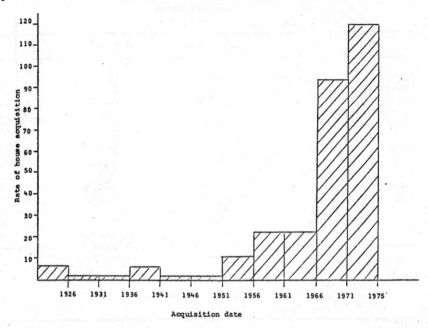

Figure 3.5   'Not decided' by acquisition date

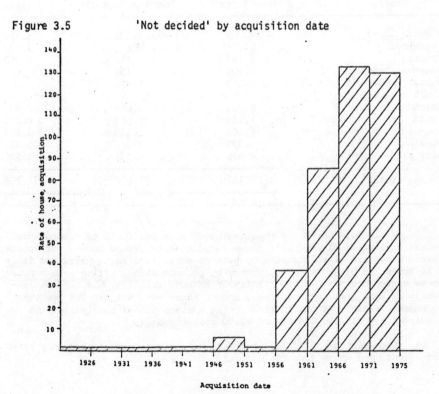

Table 3.14   Mean occupancy by owners

Nights per month

Month	Traditional	New development	Chalets
August	19.431	15.686	19.708
September	9.376	5.057	5.375
October	5.426	3.771	2.958
November/December	4.839	2.057	1.042
January/February	3.942	1.743	1.958
March	4.125	2.486	2.083
April	9.306	6.715	6.875
May	6.200	6.543	5.708
June	7.749	5.829	6.375
July	11.247	9.829	8.333
Total	81.641	59.716	60.415

Table 3.15   Mean occupancy by borrowers

Nights per month

Month	Traditional	New developments	Chalets
August	4.301	3.571	1.458
September	2.448	2.629	2.042
October	1.185	1.400	0.292
November/December	1.109	1.143	-
January/February	1.317	1.686	-
March	0.722	1.086	-
April	1.282	0.657	0.292
May	1.561	1.143	0.167
June	3.377	3.314	3.333
July	4.885	4.371	3.625
Total	22.187	21.000	11.209

Table 3.14 shows the mean occupancy rate per month of second home owners in Gwynedd divided into three categories of second home. Of course, second homes are often occupied by persons other than the owners, and Table 3.15 shows the breakdown of occupancy by persons either hiring or borrowing these second homes. It is of interest to note that 43%, 43%, and 8% respectively lent their second homes, and of these 84%, 89% and 96% received no payment except perhaps in kind. The average annual receipts of the remainder are £15.45, £24.51 and £5.00 respectively.

Summarizing Tables 3.14 and 3.15 we derive the mean occupancy rates for second home users (see Table 3.16).

Table 3.16   Mean occupancy by owners and borrowers

Nights per month

Month	Traditional	New development	Chalets
August	23.732	19.257	21.166
September	11.824	7.686	7.417
October	6.611	5.171	3.250
November/December	5.948	3.200	1.042
January/February	5.259	3.429	1.958
March	4.847	3.572	2.083
April	10.588	7.371	7.167
May	7.761	7.686	5.875
June	11.126	9.143	9.708
July	16.320	14.200	11.958
Total	103.826	80.715	71.624

Figure 3.6   Mean occupancy by owners: traditional

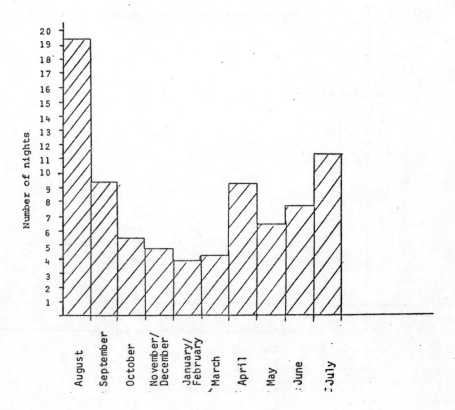

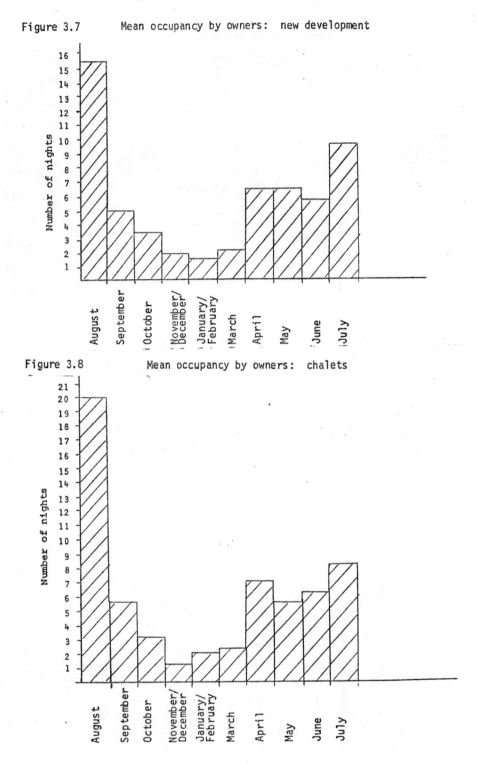

Figure 3.7   Mean occupancy by owners: new development

Figure 3.8   Mean occupancy by owners: chalets

34

Figure 3.9   Mean occupancy by borrowers: traditional

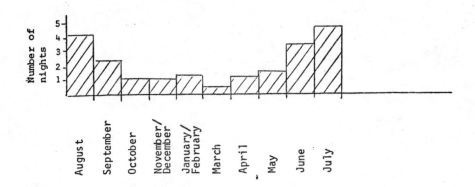

Figure 3.10.   Mean occupancy by borrowers: new development

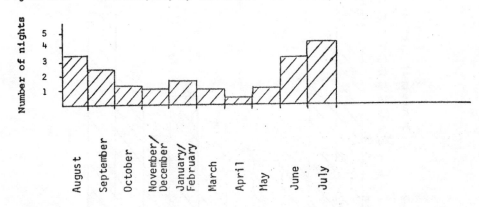

Figure 3.11   Mean occupancy by borrowers: chalets

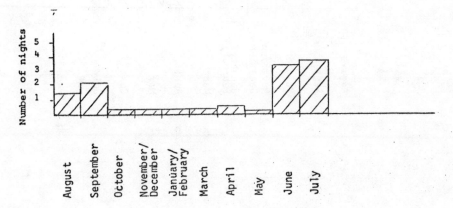

Figure 3.12   Total mean occupancy: traditional

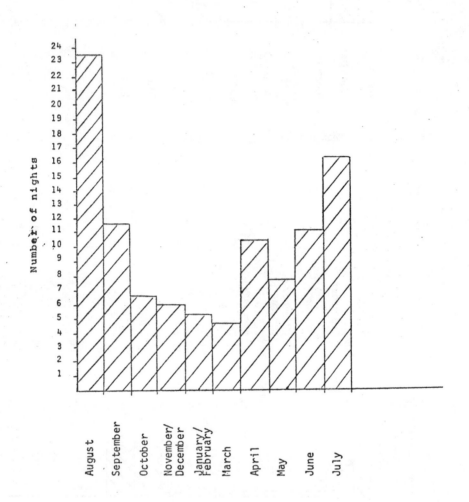

Figure 3.13   Total mean occupancy: new development

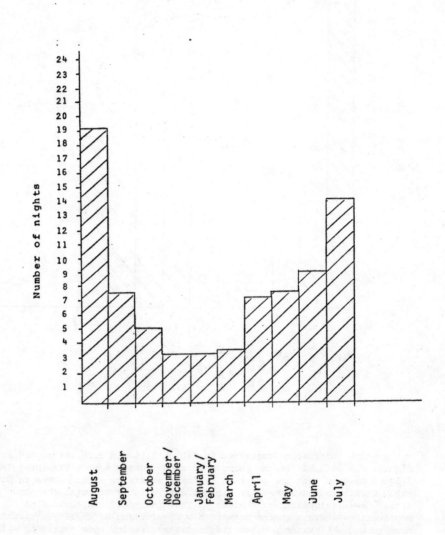

Figure 3.14   Total mean occupancy: chalets

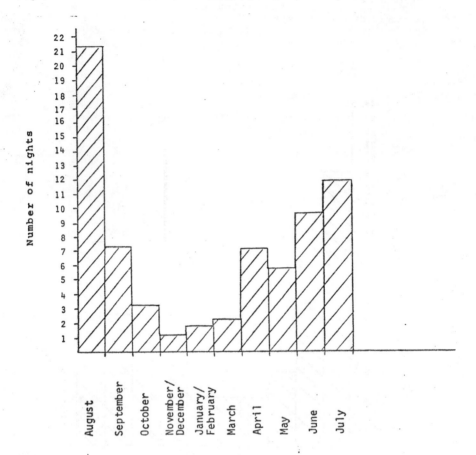

The information contained in Tables 3.14 and 3.16 is graphed in Figures 3.6 to 3.14 for the purpose of ready comparison. Examining Table 3.14 we observe that the use rate by their owners of second homes as presently structured in Gwynedd is significantly higher in total than that for either new developments or chalets. This in itself has obvious policy implications where a choice between new development or chalet construction must be made. Further, given that increased second home ownership will take place in these latter categories, the average occupancy time of second home owners may be expected to fall over time. We notice also from this table that, while the occupancy rate of all owners tends to peak in the summer months, this effect is far more pronounced in the chalet sector. The other types of property tend to have a much more even pattern of use, particularly in the case of traditional second homes.

Table 3.15 shows the use of properties by users other than the owner and his immediate family. The month by month pattern is not significantly different between traditional and new developments, but it is significantly different in the case of chalets. Whilst we should note that this may be because of site closure in the winter months, this trend is not compensated for in the summer months, with the result that total use by visitors other than the owner is approximately 50% of that of traditional and new development units.

Table 3.16 adds together the figures in Tables 3.14 and 3.15 to give total occupancy. Significantly the seasonal spread of use of traditional units is greater than that of Table 3.14, whilst the addition of visitors to the other two groups has marginally increased the polarization to the summer months in the case of new developments. Polarization has increased in the case of chalets. We find that 24% of all occupancy of traditional units takes place between 1 October and 31 March, while the respective figure for new developments is 18.5% and that for chalets 11.5%. Thus we find that in total use and seasonal spread there is a significant difference in occupancy between the three types of property.

CHAPTER FOUR

THE ECONOMIC IMPACT OF SECOND HOME
OWNERSHIP ON THE COUNTY OF GWYNEDD

Expenditure by second home owners

The details that follow of the expenditure in Gwynedd by second
home owners were obtained by an empirical survey conducted in the summer of
1974. Details of the methodology and sample framework used are given in
Chapter 7 which follows.

Table 4.1 shows expenditure per day in each of ten categories of
expenditure by type of second home. If we now multiply food shop expenditure in column 1 of Table 4.1 by the total of column 1 in Table 3.14 and
then multiply the result by the number of second homes in Gwynedd, we shall
have a total for expenditure in food shops in 1973-74 by second home owners.
Thus:

$$236.2 \times 81.641 \times 4386 = £845,786$$

Similarly Table 4.2 shows the results for our three types of second home.
Note that we have now amalgamated expenditure on souvenirs and expenditure
in non-food shops under one heading of 'expenditure in non-food shops', in
order that this information may be more readily run through the computer
model. To these totals we must add second home expenditure in each category on local government services and local labour. This gives us a total
expenditure figure for each category as in Table 4.3.

The secondary economic benefits

Thus far we have derived a total expenditure figure for second home
owners in Gwynedd, namely £2,413,310, together with separate expenditure
figures for new developments and chalets. However, this is only a measure
of the direct spending by second home owners and not the complete effect of
second home owners' spending on the economy. This section is concerned
with the overall effect of this expenditure on the economy.

Spending by second home owners has a multiplicative effect on business activity and therefore on incomes within an economy. The measurement
of this so-called multiplier should give a measure of the benefit derived
from a particular type of spending and should therefore be of use in
planning for an increase or decrease in that type of expenditure within the
economy. How then does this multiplier work and how do we measure it?

Table 4.1   Daily expenditure by category of expenditure

Pence per day

	Traditional	New developments	Chalets
Food shops	236.210	220.086	160.000
Souvenirs	8.147	7.829	19.000
Non-food shops	55.740	77.143	46.667
Hotels, public houses & cafés	113.692	154.343	94.667
Garage trade	94.355	89.571	74.208
Electricity	40.409	37.829	37.667
Gas	0.824	-	-
Rail transport	0.024	-	-
Road transport	1.317	-	-
Other services	7.105	31.514	10.958
Total	557.823	618.315	443.167

Notes: 1. Non-food shops exclude souvenir expenditure.

2. The expenditure per day figure on electricity is based on the assumption that all electricity expenditure is incurred on days of residence, for ease in grossing up.

3. The figure in column 2 (new developments) under the heading of 'other services' is significantly higher than in column 1. This is probably associated with some sporting activity around which new developments tend to be clustered.   The figure in column 3 includes expenditure by chalet owners on site rents.

Table 4.2 Expenditure by category of expenditure by type of second home

£

	Traditional	New developments	Chalets
Food shops	845,786	30,359	14,756
Non-food shops	228,774	11,721	6,056
Hotels, public houses & cafés	407,092	21,290	8,730
Garage trade	337,853	13,825	6,844
Electricity	144,689	5,839	3,474
Gas	2,948	-	-
Rail transport	877	-	-
Road transport	4,713	-	-
Other services	26,085	4,347	1,030
Total	1,998,817	87,381	40,890

Note: The figures for chalets are based on our estimate of those chalets which satisfy the ownership but not the availability criterion outlined in Chapter 6.

Table 4.3   Total expenditure by second home owners
£

	Traditional	New development	Chalets
Sub-total from Table 4.2	1,998,821	87,381	40,890
Local government services	235,254	18,689	4,670
Local labour	179,234	7,643	-
Total	2,413,310	114,230	45,757

Note: The figure for local labour under chalets has already been included in 'other services' for reasons stated earlier.

If we consider a hypothetical region which contains two firms, S, a shop, and FP, a food factory, and posit an injection, J, of £100 from purchases in S by second home owners, what will be the effect on the income of the region?   If we assume that leakages (in terms of savings, taxation, payments to firms and individuals outside the region who contribute capital or some other factor of production, etc.) constitute 10% of S's gross takings, and that 10% of the gross takings constitute his personal income, we can see that 80% of his gross takings are passed on to firm FP.   Let us further assume that FP has 10% of gross takings as leakages, as above, that 50% of FP takings are passed on to FP's labour force, and that 40% are leakages, in that they are spent outside the region on raw materials for FP.   (These flows are shown in Figure 4.1). FP labour force then spends its wages (£40) with S, inducing a further increase of £4 in S's income, £4 in leakages and £32 worth of income to FP.   The heavy lines are the first round of spending and the dotted lines are the beginning of the second round.   This process will continue through a successive number of rounds with the payments passed on becoming smaller and smaller as a result of the leakages taking place in each round, eventually diminishing to zero increase in personal incomes.   If we continue this process for three rounds and sum the totals of A, B and C, we have Table 4.4.   Thus, if we stop the process after three rounds and consider the effect of our initial injection of £100 by second home owners, we see that:

A = the direct increase in personal incomes   = £10
B = the indirect increase in personal incomes = £62.4
C = the induced increase in personal incomes = £6.24

This information may then be converted into a regional income multiplier in several ways.   Firstly, it is possible to relate the direct increase in personal incomes to the sum of the direct and the indirect personal income increase:

Direct → Direct + Indirect
  (A)   →   (A)   +   (B)
  £10   →   £10   +   £62.4 = 72.4/10 = 7.24

This is an example of a Type 1 multiplier as defined by Archer, Shea and de Vane[1], to whose work the reader may refer for a much more rigorous exposition of the concept of regional multipliers.   Alternatively, it is possible to relate the direct increase in personal incomes to the sum of

Figure 4.1   Hypothetical expenditure streams

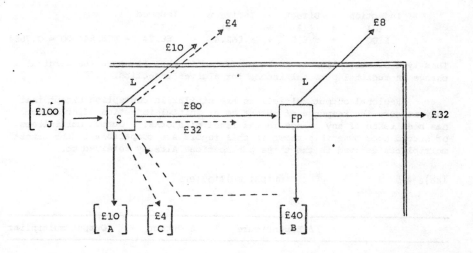

Table 4.4   Income generation
£

Round	A	B	C
1	10	40	4
2	-	16	1.6
3	-	6.4	0.64
Total	10	62.4	6.24

the direct plus indirect plus induced increase in personal incomes:

Direct	+	Direct	+	Indirect	+	Induced			
(A)	+	(A)	+	(B)	+	(C)			
£10	+	£10	+	£62.4	+	£6.24	=	78.64/10	= 7.864

This may be thought of as a Type II multiplier.[1]

Finally we may think of a multiplier which is related to the original injection and to all of the consequent changes in income. This type of multiplier, termed the 'unorthodox' multiplier[1] is the type derived for previous investigations into the economy of Anglesey by Sadler, Archer and Owen[2] and into the economy of Gwynedd[3], and the multipliers derived for second home ownership are therefore strictly comparable with these and with the tourist multipliers derived by Archer, Shea and de Vane.[1] We compare the initial injection with the sum of the direct plus indirect plus induced change in personal incomes:

$$\text{Injection} \rightarrow \text{Direct} + \text{Indirect} + \text{Induced}$$
$$(J) \rightarrow (A) + (B) + (C)$$
$$£100 \rightarrow £10 + £62.4 + £6.24 = 78.64/100 = 0.7864$$

This type of multiplier is to be preferred in that it shows the marginal change in regional personal income for a given injection.

Regional output multipliers are similar in conception except that they measure the response of output to an initial injection after account has been taken of any change in the level of stocks. Output multipliers of second home ownership shown in this report are comparable to the output multipliers derived in the three publications already referred to.

Table 4.5   Output multipliers

£

	Δ Expenditure	Δ Output	Output multiplier
Industry 1	100	140	1.40
Industry 2	200	316	1.58
Total	300	456	1.52

Before going on to calculate the second home multipliers we must mention that the derivation of these types of multipliers requires a detailed knowledge of the linkages within an economy, not only between firms and between industries within that economy, but also between output changes, income changes and consumption changes. The model used for these purposes, of which a description may be found in Chapter 8, is more fully described in Sadler, Archer and Owen.[2] The sources and methods of deriving the data are briefly described in Appendix I.

Tables 4.6 to 4.11 inclusive show the output and income multipliers for Gwynedd for three categories of property after all the effects of an increase in expenditure have been accounted for. Table 4.6 shows that the total expenditure in Gwynedd by second home owners generates a total change in output of £3,468,546. The output multiplier is thus 1.4372 for second home owners. The change in output is broken down for 23 individual sectors, showing the absolute levels of the change in output due to expenditure by second home owners, and the coefficients reduce these absolute levels to proportions.

Thus, considering row 16 of Table 4.6, we see that an injection of the £2,413,310 of second home expenditure into the economy of Gwynedd generates £435,876 of output in garage trade, or 12.57% of the total increase in output. Similarly (row 9) 5.38% of the increase in output takes place in the 'electricity' sector, being £186,530. The 'food shops' sector is responsible for the largest single increase in output, £963,750,

44

and 'food shops', 'hotels' and 'garage trade' together account for 53.34% of the increase.

Table 4.6   The output multiplier and coefficients for second home ownership in Gwynedd

£

Sector	Category: second homes	
	Δ Output	Coefficients
1. Agriculture	73,503.66	0.0212
2. Quarrying	11,593.48	0.0033
3. Engineering	2,253.67	0.0006
4. Textiles	36.76	-
5. Timber	2,967.67	0.0008
6. Other manufacturing	3,912.90	0.0011
7. Construction	53,820.47	0.0155
8. Gas	17,443.70	0.0050
9. Electricity	186,530.29	0.0538
10. Water	5,757.86	0.0017
11. Rail transport	2,293.75	0.0007
12. Road transport	15,762.89	0.0045
13. Postal & telecommunications	70,175.20	0.0202
14. Insurance, banking & finance	15,918.62	0.0046
15. Education	608.38	0.0002
16. Garage trade	435,876.75	0.1257
17. Hotels etc.	450,110.90	0.1298
18. Food shops	963,749.71	0.2779
19. Non-food shops	310,081.58	0.0894
20. Wholesalers	330,467.69	0.0953
21. Other services	215,399.43	0.0621
22. Professional & scientific	7,525.78	0.0022
23. Local government	292,755.86	0.0844
Total	3,468,546.6	1.0000

Injection J = £2,413,310   Δ Output = £3,468,546.6

$$\frac{\Sigma\Delta O}{\Sigma J} = \text{Output multiplier} = 1.4372$$

Table 4.7   The income multiplier and coefficients for
                 second home ownership in Gwynedd

£

| Sector | Category: second homes | |
	Δ Income	Coefficients
1. Agriculture	35,956.28	0.0462
2. Quarrying	6,533.66	0.0084
3. Engineering	440.97	0.0006
4. Textiles	6.51	-
5. Timber	472.93	0.0006
6. Other manufacturing	717.14	0.0009
7. Construction	18,761.05	0.0241
8. Gas	4,600.66	0.0059
9. Electricity	25,978.99	0.0334
10. Water	1,836.21	0.0024
11. Rail transport	1,596.84	0.0021
12. Road transport	7,859.13	0.0101
13. Postal & telecommunications	23,403.85	0.0301
14. Insurance, banking & finance	8,021.28	0.0103
15. Education	400.53	0.0005
16. Garage trade	46,221.70	0.0594
17. Hotels etc.	112,602,09	0.1446
18. Food shops	133,489.14	0.1715
19. Non-food shops	64,989.52	0.0835
20. Wholesalers	37,481.66	0.0481
21. Other services	133,560.74	0.1716
22. Professional & scientific	6,612.62	0.0085
23. Local government	106,940.08	0.1374
Total	778,483.58	1.0000

Injection J = £2,413,310   Δ Income = £778,483.58

$$\frac{\Sigma \Delta Y}{\Sigma J} = \text{Income multiplier} = 0.3226$$

Table 4.7 shows that the total expenditure by second home owners
generates an increase in income of £778,483.   The income multiplier is
thus 0.3226.   The first column in Table 4.7 shows the absolute amounts
received by the individual sectors, and the coefficients represent the
relative proportions of the total.   Thus row 18 shows that incomes within
the 'food shops' sector increased by £133,489, being 17.15% of the total
increase in incomes within the economy attributable to second home owners
and their families.

Notice here that, although 'garage trade' increased its output by
12.57% of the total change in output (row 16, Table 4.6), it received only
5.94% of the change in incomes.   This may be accounted for by the high

proportion of garages that are owned by firms situated outside the region, and the probability that a large proportion of the garage trade increase is provided by petrol sales. Conversely 'other services', which accounts for only 6.21% of the change in total output (row 21, Table 4.6) received 17.16% of the change in income (row 21, Table 4.7). In absolute terms the increase in output was £215,399 and the increase in income £133,561. This would suggest that the 'other services' sector is largely owned within Gwynedd, and possibly that it uses a high proportion of labour.

Tables 4.8 to 4.11 may be interpreted in a similar way. While comparison may not be made of absolute changes in the individual sectors within the three categories of property without reference to the absolute level of expenditure, the coefficients are comparable. Differences in the coefficients will represent the different expenditure patterns by the three groups and the consequently different effects that these will have on the output of each sector.

Table 4.12 shows the output and income multipliers for the three property categories. From this table we can see that the output multiplier for second homes is marginally lower than that of new developments and significantly higher than that of chalets. However, in terms of the impact on the regional economy of a given expenditure, the income multipliers are a much better guide. In this case we can see that, again, new development expenditure has the greatest impact per pound on the incomes within the region, and that expenditure by chalet owners has a significantly lower effect.

Whilst we observe that new developments show the highest output and income multipliers, we should interpret this with some caution, since new developments and chalets are both relatively new types of property. It may well be that through time the expenditure patterns for both will change. In this context the most significant difference between new developments and the other two groups appears in the income-inducing expenditure through the local authority, implying a higher rate payment by new development owners.

Finally in this chapter we must consider the size of the second home multipliers and the size of the absolute expenditure by second home owners compared with other sectors in the regional economy.

From Table 4.13 we observe that the output multiplier of second home expenditure is similar to that of the hotel sector (row 18) and ranks 16th in order of size. This implies that £1,000 injected into the second home sector will generate a larger increase in output than if it is injected into a lower ranking sector. Thus £1,000 injected into the second home sector would increase total output by £1,437; when compared with the garage trade sector, where a similar injection would increase total output by £1,118, we notice that the result differs by £319.

The income multiplier ranks 17th in magnitude and is similar to those of hotels, gas and tourism. Taking the garage trade as our example we see that £1,000 increase in expenditure will increase incomes in the garage trade by £133, compared with £323 in the case of second homes, a difference of £190.

In absolute terms, the expenditure by second home owners ranks 18th in magnitude in Table 4.13. Such activities as quarrying, textiles and water have lower total outputs, although not necessarily lower multipliers.

47

Table 4. 8   The output multiplier and coefficients for
new developments in Gwynedd

£

Sector	Category: new developments	
	Δ Output	Coefficients
1. Agriculture	2,966.85	0.0180
2. Quarrying	748.78	0.0045
3. Engineering	99.05	0.0006
4. Textiles	1.75	–
5. Timber	181.03	0.0011
6. Other manufacturing	190.30	0.0011
7. Construction	3,292.40	0.0200
8. Gas	796.02	0.0048
9. Electricity	7,938.86	0.0482
10. Water	290.30	0.0018
11. Rail transport	72.46	0.0004
12. Road transport	601.11	0.0036
13. Postal & telecommunications	3,567.21	0.0216
14. Insurance, banking & finance	683.06	0.0041
15. Education	29.43	0.0002
16. Garage trade	18,844.30	0.1143
17. Hotels etc.	23,513.39	0.1427
18. Food shops	36,527.84	0.2217
19. Non-food shops	15,961.69	0.0969
20. Wholesalers	13,400.91	0.0813
21. Other services	13,034.03	0.0791
22. Professional & scientific	389.09	0.0024
23. Local government	21,657.39	0.1314
Total	164,787.25	1.0000

Injection J = £114,229.55   Δ Output = £164,787.25

$$\frac{\Sigma \Delta O}{\Sigma J} = \text{Output multiplier} = 1.4426$$

Table 4.9   The income multiplier and coefficients for
new developments in Gwynedd

£

Sector	Category: new developments	
	Δ Income	Coefficients
1. Agriculture	1,463.09	0.0361
2. Quarrying	421.98	0.0104
3. Engineering	19.31	0.0005
4. Textiles	0.30	-
5. Timber	28.85	0.0007
6. Other manufacturing	34.98	0.0009
7. Construction	1,147.62	0.0283
8. Gas	209.91	0.0052
9. Electricity	1,105.63	0.0273
10. Water	92.58	0.0023
11. Rail transport	50.43	0.0012
12. Road transport	299.72	0.0074
13. Postal & telecommunications	1,189.20	0.0293
14. Insurance, banking & finance	344.19	0.0085
15. Education	19.43	0.0005
16. Garage trade	1,998.31	0.0493
17. Hotels etc.	5,882.31	0.1450
18. Food shops	5,059.41	0.1247
19. Non-food shops	3,345.75	0.0825
20. Wholesalers	1,519.79	0.0375
21. Other services	8,083.91	0.1993
22. Professional & scientific	341.85	0.0084
23. Local government	7,899.64	0.1948
Total	40,558.19	1.0000

Injection J = £114,229.55 ΔY = £40,558.19

$\frac{\Sigma \Delta Y}{\Sigma J}$ = Income multiplier = 0.3551

Table 4.10   The output multiplier and coefficients for
chalets in Gwynedd

£

Sector	Category: chalets	
	Δ Output	Coefficients
1. Agriculture	8,267.01	0.0211
2. Quarrying	1,173.20	0.0030
3. Engineering	290.90	0.0007
4. Textiles	3.62	–
5. Timber	328.18	0.0008
6. Other manufacturing	419.15	0.0010
7. Construction	5,990.64	0.0153
8. Gas	1,490.75	0.0038
9. Electricity	26,049.72	0.0667
10. Water	675.49	0.0017
11. Rail transport	155.54	0.0004
12. Road transport	1,293.64	0.0033
13. Postal & telecommunications	7,419.06	0.0190
14. Insurance, banking & finance	1,836.74	0.0047
15. Education	68.96	0.0002
16. Garage trade	53,046.14	0.1356
17. Hotels etc.	58,850.08	0.1505
18. Food shops	103,801.59	0.2655
19. Non-food shops	45,940.98	0.1175
20. Wholesalers	37,377.61	0.0956
21. Other services	7,445.05	0.0190
22. Professional & scientific	768.74	0.0020
23. Local government	28,331.20	0.0724
Total	391,023.99	1.0000

Injection J = £276,004.51   Δ Output = £391,023.99

$$\frac{\Sigma \Delta O}{\Sigma J} = \text{Output multiplier} = 1.4167$$

Table 4.11   The income multiplier and coefficients for
chalets in Gwynedd

£

Sector	Category: chalets	
	Δ Income	Coefficients
1. Agriculture	4,065.14	0.0511
2. Quarrying	661.20	0.0083
3. Engineering	56.69	0.0007
4. Textiles	0.60	-
5. Timber	52.25	0.0006
6. Other manufacturing	76.63	0.0010
7. Construction	2,088.20	0.0262
8. Gas	393.20	0.0049
9. Electricity	3,628.23	0.0456
10. Water	215.42	0.0027
11. Rail transport	108.28	0.0014
12. Road transport	567.40	0.0071
13. Postal & telecommunications	2,475.22	0.0311
14. Insurance, banking & finance	925.66	0.0116
15. Education	45.42	0.0006
16. Garage trade	5,625.26	0.0707
17. Hotels etc.	14,722.19	0.1850
18. Food shops	14,377.56	0.1806
19. Non-food shops	9,630.08	0.1210
20. Wholesalers	4,239.49	0.0532
21. Other services	4,603.80	0.0578
22. Professional & scientific	675.68	0.0085
23. Local government	10,352.87	0.1301
Total	79,586.37 [*]	1.0000

Injection J = £276,004.51   Δ Income = £79,586.37

$$\frac{\Sigma \Delta Y}{\Sigma J} = \text{Income multiplier} = 0.2884$$

[*] This is the change in income as a result of an injection of £276,004.51,
i.e. spending by chalet families totalling 947. Use of these figures
should not be made without reference to Chapter 7. The income multiplier
and coefficients are, of course, unchanged no matter what the size of the
injection.

Table 4.12   Output and income multipliers

Category	Output multiplier	Income multiplier
Second homes	1.4372	0.3226
New developments	1.4426	0.3551
Chalets	1.4167	0.2884

Table 4.13   Output and income multipliers: Gwynedd

Sector	Output multiplier	Income multiplier
1. Agriculture	1.802	0.694
2. Quarrying	1.700	0.741
3. Engineering	1.206	0.239
4. Textiles	1.141	0.201
5. Timber	1.243	0.214
6. Other manufacturing	1.381	0.299
7. Construction	1.732	0.557
8. Gas	1.385	0.349
9. Electricity	1.186	0.182
10. Water	1.402	0.423
11. Rail transport	1.754	0.891
12. Road transport	1.602	0.643
13. Ports	1.971	1.212
14. Postal & telecommunications	1.273	0.397
15. Insurance, banking & finance	1.578	0.647
16. Education	1.559	0.789
17. Garage trade	1.118	0.133
18. Hotels etc.	1.457	0.359
19. Food shops	1.567	0.256
20. Non-food shops	1.374	0.286
21. Wholesalers	1.511	0.288
22. Other services	1.528	0.747
23. Professional & scientific	1.813	1.082
24. Local government	1.537	0.505
25. National government	1.325	0.449
26. Defence	1.470	0.505
27. Tourism	1.158	0.368
Second homes	1.437	0.323

References

1. P. G. Sadler, B. H. Archer & C. B. Owen, *Regional Income Multipliers*, Bangor Occasional Papers in Economics No.1, University of Wales Press, Cardiff, 1973.

2. P. G. Sadler, B. H. Archer & R. D. J. de Vane, *The Gwynedd Study*, report to the Gwynedd County Council, 1974.

3. B. H. Archer, S. Shea & R. D. J. de Vane, *Tourism in Gwynedd: an Economic Study*, Wales Tourist Board, 1974.

CHAPTER FIVE

SECOND HOME OWNERSHIP AND HOUSE PRICES

Over the past five years a controversy has erupted over second home
ownership.   This is based to a large extent on a combination of the effect
of second home ownership on the cultural activities and customs of communities whose background is different from that of the second home owners,
the effect on village life, and the problems that high house prices
represent to young local people.   In this chapter we shall attempt to
isolate the 'house price' problem and see to what extent second home ownership tends to increase house prices.

Initially we approached the problem by attempting to compare two
similar areas, one with a high density of second homes, the other with a
low density, and to compare relative house prices for similar dwellings.
This posed many problems.   Whilst it is possible to be fairly definite
in terms of the comparability of the physical structure of a range of
houses, it is much more difficult to measure the comparability of physical
amenities such as access to public transport, shops and the sea.   Again,
comparison of views, climate and community closeness becomes difficult to
make.   This leads one into the problem of what are similar areas.

In an area like Gwynedd, sub-areas are very dissimilar in that the
industrial development has taken place in pockets.   Similarly, the coast-
line ranges from cliff face to vast sandy beaches.   Given that one could
find an area with the same type of industrial structure, in that the
required labour force was similar in age and skill, and received similar
remuneration, it would be necessary coincidentally to discover another
area which had the same type of labour supply.   A further problem arises
in that the types of industries prevalent in Gwynedd, e.g. power stations
and large factories, require a relative large labour force per unit.   If
we extend our area to include the residence of a high proportion of those
employed in this type of activity, given, of course, that we have knowledge
of journey to work times and distances, we find that our area increases to
such an extent as to negate any potential differences in house prices.

In sum then we were seeking two areas with similar amenities,
geographical location, housing structure, industrial mix and labour force,
but with differing densities of second home ownership.   We considered two
parishes, Aberffraw and Llanengan to be the most comparable, but, given
the lack of exact data for these two parishes, the difference in the
density of second home ownership appeared insignificant after statistically
controlling for the facility of sailing at Llanengan which was lacking at
Aberffraw.   Further, in this context, one has to consider the available
housing supply, which requires a detailed knowledge of council house numbers
and private estate holdings.

We concluded that, given the similarity of house prices in the coastal area, after controlling for amenities, and the fact that there was no statistically significant difference in second home density after controlling for these amenities, the only remaining approach from the micro point of view was a comparison between all coastal and all inland areas.

Certainly we found that the density of second home ownership tended to be lower in the inland areas, and that, in general, house prices tended to be lower. However, there was no means of comparing the different areas in a meaningful way, since we found it impossible to put a value on the industrial differences (most activity is on or near the coast, and even the agricultural activity is dissimilar), the transport facilities (most of the better routes are coastal), or the different wage rates.

This then leaves a macro approach to the problem. We approached this by considering what proportion of the demand for housing is attributable to the demand for a second home.

Building society statistics for England and Wales suggest that houses tend to change hands once every seven years. Applying this figure to Gwynedd, which has a total of 75,642 dwellings (from local authority data), we should expect that last year some 10,800 houses would have changed hands in Gwynedd. At the same time we know from Table 2.13 that the average number of second homes acquired in each of the last three years is 365, or 3.37% of all houses changing hands in each year.

This is a little unrealistic, however, since the building society figures include urban areas, where there is traditionally greater mobility. Table 5.1 shows the houses taken up by second home owners over a range of house turnover possibilities. We make no attempt to make predictions from this information, since we have no data on the rate of house turnover in Gwynedd. It would be possible to derive this information either by a study of each individual rate book, isolating those houses which changed hands in a given year, or alternatively by a study of the list of electors and year to year changes thereof. This latter would be an inferior method, since new entrants into an area do not necessarily elect in that area.

Table 5.1   Second home take-up by house turnover

Postulated rate of turnover Years	Number of second homes purchased	Number of all homes purchased	% of second home purchases per year
7	365	10,806	3.37
14	365	5,403	6.75
21	365	3,602	10.13
28	365	2,702	13.51
35	365	2,161	16.89
42	365	1,801	20.26
49	365	1,544	23.63

We also attempted to examine the difference between relative house prices within and outside Gwynedd. Unfortunately we were once again hampered by lack of data. The only source of data on house prices, furnished by one of the major building societies, gives only a breakdown into regions, of which Wales is one, and this only starts from the last quarter of 1971. Furthermore, it is based on new and existing properties mortgaged to that building society.   However, it does suggest that, after the North East and Northern Ireland, house prices in Wales are the lowest, and that the rate of change in house prices in that period approached the average for the United Kingdom.

Thus, because of insufficient data, we feel unable to many any predictions of the effect of second home ownership on house prices.   It may well be that the market for primary and secondary homes is, in fact, not one but two markets, with only a slight ratchet effect between the two. It may well be the case that, except in fairly specific instances where a particular facility is available, further increases in income of the indig- enous population will result in greater rural nucleation, and therefore further separation of the markets.   (In this context see J. Chr. Hansen, 'The problem of marginal areas in Norway, population trends and prospects', *Meddelelser Fra Geografisk Institutt Ved Norges Handelshøyskole og Univer- sitetet i Bergen*, No.19.)   However, it is probable that any further second home ownership will take place largely in the form of new developments.

Conclusions

The present structure of second home ownership within the county of Gwynedd resulted in an expenditure of £2,413,310 at 1974 prices.   This generated total business turnover of £3,468,546 and created personal house- hold income amounting to £778,483.   This compares favourably with such sectors as textiles, quarrying and rail transport, and puts the second home industry about mid-way in the income-producing league.

However, as noted earlier, with the supply of 'traditional' second homes drying up, the future tendency will probably be towards purpose-built new development houses as second homes.   These have both higher output multipliers and higher income multipliers than 'traditional' second homes, and a considerably higher income multiplier compared with chalets.   Refer- ence should be made not only to the relevant multipliers, but also to expenditure per day and occupancy rates when planning for the future growth or decline in second home ownership.

CHAPTER SIX

DEFINITIONS AND CONCEPTS

In order to investigate some of the actual and potential effects of second home ownership it is necessary to define the term 'second home'. A working definition is above all necessary in order that valid comparisons may be made between present and future research findings. Obviously the definition used depends upon the particular problem under review, and this could result, therefore, in more than one definition of second homes. It may well be that a cost-benefit approach would require a totally different definition from an investigation into the effects of second home ownership on house prices. Again, an investigation into the variables affecting the present demand for second homes may well require a different definition from an investigation into the past or future determinants of demand.

Before going on to examine some of the definitions which have been used in economic and social investigations of second home ownership, it is useful to examine what types of property may be encompassed within the term second home.

Effectively, any inhabitable area may be thought of as *home*. Similarly, *a home* is simply a confined area, which may range from caves in some areas of France to tents in North Africa, where these fulfil the same function.

The Oxford Dictionary defines:

Home: dwelling place; fixed residence or family or household; native land.

Dwelling: place of residence; house.

House: building for human habitation or occupation.

Thus, a home may be any inhabitable area, and a special case of this is a house, which is required to be of some form of material construction. If we assume that any inhabited area which imposes barriers against the elements may be thought of as home, and if we may assume that any home may become a second home, then accordingly we may list:

(a) houses
(b) hotels, inns, boarding houses
(c) flats
(d) chalets
(e) caravans
(f) boats

as possible or potential second homes in the United Kingdom.

Given that these all form potential second homes, we can approach a definition from three angles:

(1)   from the point of view of the structure of the property
(2)   from the point of view of ownership of the property
(3)   from the point of view of occupation of the property.

Before investigating these approaches, we shall examine some of the extant definitions of second homes.   It should be borne in mind that, in many articles not mentioned here, it seems to be assumed that the reader understands intuitively what constitutes a second home or, in the case of the United States of America, a holiday home.

The Wye College Report on Second Homes[1] adopted at the outset of the study a definition of a second home as 'a property which is the occasional residence of a household that usually lives elsewhere and which is primarily used for recreational purposes'.   The original scope of the enquiry included country cottages, seaside houses and flats, houseboats and stationary caravans, but it was not intended to cover city properties. The report accepts that its definition does not, in fact, specify actual ownership, since far more people use second homes than actually own them. However, the data sources, namely (a) the rate demands which are sent to addresses outside a local authority area, (b) the personal knowledge of rating officers, (c) electoral registers, which mark owners of property with a permanent residence elsewhere as 'L' voters, and (d) planning permission and improvement grant applications, are all geared to finding the number of homes used as second homes, and not the number of second home owners.

A Countryside Commission report,[5] which was largely based on the Wye College study, uses the same definition.   In the Pilot National Recreation Survey[2] second homes were identified as 'another house, cottage, bungalow, etc. for your own family use', which tends to beg the question of caravans, chalets and houseboats.

Hugh D. Clout, in his work *Second Homes in France*[4] used the 1962 French Census definition, 'homes which owners occupy for only a short period of the year, including holiday homes and furnished flats used for tourist purposes, but excluding hotels', which once again tends to ignore the problems of caravan and boat ownership.

The Denbighshire second home report[6] states on page 5: 'No attempt was made in the questionnaire or covering letter to define a second home. Because the pattern of use might vary widely, it was unwise to delineate a "second home" too narrowly;   instead it was implicit in the text that it was a dwelling intended mainly for leisure or holiday purposes, and was not the usual or permanent place of residence of the owner'.   The Denbighshire investigation confined itself to rural cottages and purpose-built second homes, ignoring caravans and boats.

The Caernarvonshire second home report[3] used as a definition: 'A dwelling used by its owners and possibly other visitors for leisure or holiday purposes and which is not the usual or permanent residence of the owner'.   The report also provided definitions of:

(a)   *a holiday investment property* being 'a dwelling owned either locally or outside the county and not permanently occupied, but let to holiday-makers solely on a commercial basis';

(b)   *club/institute/company holiday property* being 'similar to above, but used only by club members or company employees and clients'.

The investigation covers only second homes proper; excluded are properties owned outside the county and permanently occupied by local residents, investment properties let on a solely commercial basis for holidays, and club/institute/company properties hired to members.

The Merioneth Structure Plan report on second homes[7] states on page 2: 'For the purposes of this report a second home is defined as a dwelling used by a family primarily for recreation and leisure purposes as distinct from a first home which forms the normal domicile of the family from which they travel to work or school.   Apart from permanent buildings, many static caravans are used as second homes, but in this report consideration is generally restricted to permanent dwellings, or semi-permanent development such as wooden chalets.   Accommodation used primarily for letting on a commercial basis for holiday purposes is also excluded'.

The last three definitions are all moving towards a concept of a second home as a static physical structure, the primary function of which is to provide a recreation base for a family, and which is not its sole residence.   The three approaches towards a definition outlined earlier, i.e. from the point of view of (1) the structure of the property, (2) the ownership of the property, (3) the occupation of the property, may be thought of as the means of investigating the three major economic questions posed by the ownership of second accommodation units, namely:

1.   the problem of predicting and assessing the structure now and future demand and supply of dwelling units within a region;

2.   the use to which these properties may be put for the purposes of predicting transport requirements, service requirements in general and available accommodation for predicted labour force levels;

3.   whether, in fact, ownership should be encouraged or restricted, in view of the benefits and costs which apply within the region.

Accordingly we shall set out three different definitions.

(a)   *A second accommodation unit*: any accommodation unit which is capable of being used as a dwelling for a period of the year and which is owned by a private individual or corporation who already owns another dwelling.

(b)   *A second house*: (a special case of (a) above) a permanent static structure which is capable of being used as a dwelling for twelve months of the year and is owned by a private individual or corporation who already owns another dwelling.

(c)   *A second home*: any static accommodation unit which may be owned, leased or rented, and which is available for the exclusive use over a twelve-month period of a family unit whose normal daily journey time is minimized at another residence.

We must now examine into which categories each of our own types of units falls.

(1)   *A second accommodation unit*.   This may encompass private houses, hotels, inns, boarding houses, flats, chalets, static caravans and static

boats owned by a private individual who already owns another accommodation unit, although not necessarily of the same type. Notice that here we are not concerned with the type of use made of the stock of accommodation, but solely with its existence; neither are we requiring any rate of use of the accommodation unit. However, if we were required to assess, for example, the available tourist accommodation, we should require to know the detailed structure of the accommodation units, their availability for use, and some measure of their size. In passing, we note that measurement of size is usually by bedspace, and that a consistently applied definition of bedspace would be useful for comparison of all types of 'visitor' research.

(2) A second house. This is a special case of an accommodation unit in that it is (i) required to be of material construction, (ii) static, (iii) capable of being used as an accommodation unit throughout a twelve-month period. Here we are ruling out all types of accommodation, including chalets, other than houses. We are also not requiring any qualification of journey time minimization, in that a second house may be in a position of minimal normal daily journey time, and still not be used or qualify as a second home. What we are attempting to identify is the property which is owned for investment purposes, and which may be either empty or let out to local residents on a temporary or permanent basis. Only if the property is visited by the owner for more than maintenance or rent collecting purposes may it be thought of as a second home.

(3) A second home. We shall examine in turn each of our known types of accommodation unit to identify which may be thought of as a second home. For a private house to fall into the category of second home it must be a house which is owned, leased, or rented, and which is available for the exclusive use, over a twelve-month period, of a family unit whose normal daily journey time is minimized at another residence. Notice here that we are not requiring that a family unit shall own its primary residence, simply that its normal daily journey time shall be less than it would be in its alternative accommodation. Also we are not requiring exclusive use, but only the availability of exclusive use if the family so desires. Thus we do not rule out letting or sub-letting to friends or tourists.

We may exclude from the category 'second home' council houses, which are not available for use as second homes, and also private houses owned by clubs and organizations, including corporations. These may be looked upon as second houses in that their function may be regarded as an investment geared to (a) capital gain and/or (b) the wellbeing of members or employees.

Hotels, inns and boarding houses do not fall into the category of second home since they do not provide availability of exclusive use.

Flats, which may be thought of as houses within houses, will fall into the category of second homes, provided that they are available for exclusive use throughout the twelve-month period. Chalets and static caravans will only fall into the category of second homes if the availability criterion is satisfied, and touring caravans will be excluded in that they fail to satisfy the static criterion. Houseboats which are affixed to a permanent mooring will be included provided they satisfy the availability criterion.

References

1. C. L. Bielckus *et al., Second Homes in England and Wales*, Countryside Planning Unit, School of Rural Economics and Related Studies, Wye College, London, 1972.

2. British Travel Association/University of Keele, *Pilot National Recreation Survey: Report No.1*, 1967.

3. Caernarvonshire County Planning Department, *Second Homes*, Caernarvon, 1973.

4. Hugh D. Clout, 'Second homes in France', *Journal of the Town Planning Institute*, 55, October 1969, pp.440-443.

5. Dartington Amenity Research Trust, *Second Homes in England and Wales*, DART publication No.7, Totnes, 1972.

6. Denbighshire County Planning Department, *Second Homes in Denbighshire*, Ruthin, 1972.

7. Merioneth County Council, *The Merioneth Structure Plan - Subject Report No.17, Second Homes*, Dolgellau, 1973.

CHAPTER SEVEN

THE EMPIRICAL SURVEY

Data sources

Section 1: caravans as second homes

We considered first the problem of caravans. According to our definition a caravan may be a second home if it is static and available for exclusive use for a twelve month period. There are four types to consider:

(a) Static caravans within the curtilage of a house. It is impossible for these to be second homes since planning approval is only given on the grounds of use by the household which occupies the house. Thus it would be possible for a single static caravan within the curtilage of a house to be part of a second home, if such a house were a second home, but it would be unrealistic to regard it as a second home in its own right.

(b) Static caravans on non-residential sites. It is the policy of Gwynedd County Council to restrict use of caravans, except on residential sites, to normal holiday periods. Pre-1960 planning permission was a little more fluid in that the stipulation on occupancy was not necessarily a specific time period but generally that the site was not to be a residential site. While there is little doubt that a minority of caravans in this category are occupied, or capable of being occupied, throughout the year, the number would appear to be minimal and the costs and problems involved in assessing that number high. Thus it was decided to exclude this type of caravan from the second home population.

(c) Static caravans on residential sites. These fulfil all the requirements of the second home definition and accordingly are included.

(d) Other static caravans. There is a limited number in Caernarvonshire and Merioneth.

We derived the totals of caravans in the above categories by direct reference to the planning authorities concerned. It would have been possible to obtain a total of all caravans from the rating register and direct enquiry at the addresses listed, but this would have been time-consuming and expensive. A far better estimate was available from the planning authorities, especially with regard to the difference between (a) static caravans within the curtilage of a house and (d) other static caravans, which are usually on single sites in the proximity of houses.

Section 2: houses as second homes

In theory all houses in Gwynedd may be second homes, and it would

have been possible to take a 10% sample of the 73,505 homes to establish
which were second homes.   In view of the time and expense involved it was
necessary to narrow down the potential second home population.   Possible
data sources in this respect are:

(1)   the rates books
(2)   the local Rating Officers
(3)   electoral registers
(4)   planning permission, mortgage and improvement grant applications.

Because of resource limitations it was decided to use a combination
of (1) and (2) above to establish a control total.   This method has been
used by various county planning authorities in North Wales.   Two problems
arise here.   In the first place the total will include houses which are
not second homes, e.g. in the situation where a resident has his rates paid
by a trust or bank or other agent who is outside the county.   Secondly, it
will not necessarily include those second home owners who have their rate
demands sent direct to the second home.

The first problem is not difficult to solve because the survey
returns will enable those homes which are not second homes to be excluded.
The second problem is rather more difficult.   Some work has been done on
this by Caernarvonshire Planning Department and Merioneth Planning Department
within Gwynedd.   Certain parishes were taken and studied in detail, using
the rating registers and local information, and the general consensus of
opinion is that the rating register in this respect underestimates by about
20%.   In our detailed analysis of four parishes, which was carried out
concurrently with this investigation, we were able to assess whether this
was, in fact, the order of magnitude.   However, it does introduce a possible area of bias in that the (suspected) 20% may not manifest the same
expenditure patterns as the remainder.   Whether there is a significant bias
was ascertained from the detailed survey.

Section 3: chalets as second homes

We derived the total of chalets in Gwynedd by direct reference to
the relevant district planning authorities.   Of the total of 947 chalets
18 were usable throughout a twelve-month period, and were accordingly
included in our sample population as potential second homes.

The policy applied to chalets varied widely between the original
pre-1974 county authorities.   Anglesey (Ynys Môn) did not encourage chalet
development, and there are only a few pre-1947 Town and Country Planning
Act chalets on the island.   Merioneth appears to have viewed chalets as
an upgrading of the caravan sector, and accordingly most of the chalets
within Merioneth have the same occupancy restrictions on them as do the
caravans.   Caernarvonshire appears to have considered them as a development which provided tourist accommodation of a fairly permanent nature, and
a type of second home which took the pressure off house prices.   However,
probably with a view to retaining the cultural traditions of rural North
Wales, either the structure of the accommodation unit or, alternatively, an
occupancy constraint has ensured that the majority are not available for
year-round use.

Section 4: new developments

In certain strategic places in Gwynedd new developments have taken
place which appear to cater almost exclusively for the tourist or second

home owner.   These are generally self-contained groups of houses built
around a recreational activity.   Our sample population was once again
drawn from the relevant rate books and the planning authorities concerned.
There are 231 at present and according to whether or not occupancy restrictions apply these fall within or without our definition of a second home.

The sampling framework

In sum then we had four distinct types of potential second home,
giving a total of 7,105 in all.   Of these some 6,963 were houses constructed of traditional materials, and they constituted some 98% of our sample
population.   A problem which we envisaged was objections to our definitions
of a second home, and therefore a request by planners for information on,
perhaps, houses used as second homes plus all chalets, or chalets and
caravans.   Since we already had information on the expenditure pattern and
occupancy rates of non-residential caravan owners, this would require us to
produce expenditure patterns and occupancy rates for all chalet owners and
new development owners apart from those which fell within our definition.

Since four different questionnaires would have to be used we
decided to approach the problem as four different surveys.

Survey A

This covered accommodation units constructed of traditional materials which were not new developments but otherwise satisfied our criteria
of a second home.   We divided the 6,963 second homes in this category into
class intervals by density of second home ownership, as shown in Tables
7.1 to 7.3, and summed the absolute totals in each class, as shown in
Table 7.4.

Using the formula

$$n = \frac{z^2 b^2}{e^2}$$

where n is the sample size, z is 1.96 (since the confidence coefficient is
0.95), e is half the confidence interval, and b is the standard deviation,
we calculated that a 10% random sample with a response rate of 38% would
give us an expenditure error of less than 8% which would be adequate for
our purposes.   At this point we came up against the time and financial
constraints of collecting 7,105 names, addresses and rateable values.
Since this was impracticable, we selected the required number of second
homes in each class interval by selecting parishes at random until we had
sufficient second homes.   The parishes selected for the sample are shown
in Table 7.5.   Where only part of a parish was used, the names and addresses of the required number were selected at random from the potential
second home population as shown by the rates book.   For these purposes
all hereditaments which incurred rates paid from another address were
deemed to be potential second homes.

Survey B: residential caravans

Since there were only 65 residential caravans known to the regul-
ating authorities, and these were clustered on 6 sites, we decided to do a

100% sample in order to get a reliable estimate of expenditure patterns. This survey was run concurrently with Survey A.

Survey C: chalets

This was divided into two parts. We determined to survey 100% of the potential second homes, i.e. those with all-year availability of use, plus a 15% sample of all other chalets. The method of selecting the other chalets was random.

Survey D: new developments

There are 231 new development houses. We surveyed 20% of new development houses in order that we should have a meaningful result (at Portdinorwic, Porthmadog, Tywyn and Abersoch).

Thus far we had been identifying our potential second home population from the rates book, where an address of the ratepayer other than the address of the property which incurs the rate denotes a potential second home. In order to identify those second homes which had their rate demands sent to the second home we determined on a one hundred percent sample of four parishes. Since we knew the expected number, the actual would give us a grossing up percentage for the other parishes.

The parishes selected for the expenditure survey are shown in Table 7.6. Aberffraw, Llanengan, Llangower, Llanymawddwy were chosen for the one hundred percent sample.

We were interested in the effect of second home ownership on house prices and therefore picked Aberffraw and Llanengan as two parishes which manifested similar geographical features but significantly different densities of second home ownership. These are both coastal parishes and so we selected two inland parishes to get a balanced viewpoint. Llangower and Llanymawddwy are adjacent parishes in Merioneth which, according to the planning authority, manifest significantly different second home densities.

Names and addresses of potential second home owners, together with the locations of the accommodation units incurring the rates, were collected by personal examination of the rates books of each relevant authority, except where this information was available as a computer print off.

The empirical survey

In order to get as good a cross section of second home users as possible, the survey period was from mid-July to mid-September, and two visits were made to each property. In the event of non-contact after these visits a questionnaire was left, together with a covering letter and pre-paid envelope, for completion by 16 September 1974.

We achieved a 71% response rate overall, and the response rate where actual contact was made with the second home owner was well over 90%. Surprisingly the response rate for questionnaires left at the second home was almost 50%.

Table 7.1   Class distribution of density of second homes as a

Class A: 0.0-9.9%		Class B: 10.0-19.9%	
Parish	No. of second homes	Parish	No. of second homes
Aberffraw	20	Bodwrog	15
Trefdraeth	12	Cerrigceinwen	29
Pentraeth	16	Llantrisant	8
Penmynydd	3	Llangenedl	75
Llansadwrn	2	Llanddona	24
Newborough	13	Carreglefn	4
Llanidan	8	Llanfair M.E.	92
Llangristiolus	9	Penrhoslligwy	12
Llangoed	25		
Llangeinwen	9		
Llangadwaladr	5		
Llangaffo	4		
Llaniestyn Rural	1		
Llandaniel Fab.	5		
Llandegfan	40		
Llanfairpwll	1		
Llanfihangel	8		
Llanallgo	30		
Llanddyfnan	8		
Llaneilian	26		
Llanfechell	15		
Llanbadrig	35		
Llandyfrydog	12		
Llangwyllog	1		
Rhosybol	8		
Llanfihangel T.B.	2		
Llanerchymedd	1		
Llanfairynghornwy	8		
Rhodogeido	2		
Llecheynfarnwy	2		
Amlwch U.D.	118		
Beaumaris M.B.	44		
Menai Bridge	6		
	499		259

Anglesey total

percentage of homes within each parish: Anglesey

Class C: 20.0-29.9%		Class D: 30.0% & over	
Parish	No. of second homes	Parish	No. of second homes
Bodedern	78	Holyhead Rural	298
Heneglwys	24	Llandrygarn	21
Llandeusant	35	Llanfaelog	293
Llanfachraeth	37	Llanrhyddlad	72
Llanfaethlu	45	Rhoscolyn	75
Llanfairynneubol	24		
Llechylched	59		
Trewalchmai	63		
Llaneugrad	28		
	393		759

- 1,910

Table 7.2   Class distribution of density of second homes as a

Class A: 0.0-9.9%		Class B: 10.0-19.9%	
Parish	No. of second homes	Parish	No. of second homes
Bethesda	72	Clynnog	54
Betws-y-Coed	15	Llanberis	75
Conwy	86	Llandeiniolen	184
Criccieth	21	Llandwrog	125
Llandudno	116	Llanrug	117
Llanfairfechan	54	Waenfawr	72
Penmaenmawr	64	Botwnnog	51
Portmadoc	103	Buan	21
Pwllheli	46	Dolbenmaen	72
Llanfaglan	2	Dolwyddelan	24
Llanfairisgaer	33	Llanrhychwyn	9
Llanllyfni	129		
Llanwnda	48		
Llanaelhaiarn	46		
Llannor	33		
Llanystumdwy	51		
Caerhun	25		
Capel Curig	9		
Henryd	3		
Maenan	4		
Trefriw	6		
Aber	1		
Llanllechid	13		
Llandegai	6		
Pentir	11		
	997		804

Caernarvonshire

percentage of homes within each parish: Caernarvonshire

Class C: 20.0-29.9%		Class D: 30.0% & over	
Parish	No. of second homes	Parish	No. of second homes
Aberdaron	91	Beddgelert	91
Nefyn	209	Betws Garmon	41
Pistyll	48	Llanbedrog	119
Tudweiliog	63	Llanengan	419
		Penmachno	102
	411		772

Total - 2,984

Table 7.3   Class distribution of density of second homes as a

Class A: 0.0-9.9%		Class B: 10.0-19.9%	
Parish	No. of second homes	Parish	No. of second homes
Bala	13	Barmouth	94
Dolgellau	49	Llanbedr	25
Ffestiniog	148	Llanfair	23
Penrhyndeudraeth	48	Maentwrog	35
Llanegryn	4	Trawsfynydd	65
Llanymawddwy	2	Brithdir	44
		Llanddwywe-is-y-graig	17
		Llanddwywe-uwch-y-graig	4
		Llanelltyd	28
		Llanfachraeth	34
		Llandderfel	31
		Llanfor	42
		Llanuwchllyn	37
		Llanycil	34
	264		513

Merioneth

Table 7.4   Class distribution of density of second homes: Gwynedd

County	Class A 0.0-9.9%	Class B 10.0-19.9%	Class C 20.0-29.9%	Class D 30.0% & over
Anglesey	499	259	393	759
Caernarvonshire	997	804	411	772
Merioneth	264	513	1,001	291
Totals	1,760	1,576	1,805	1,822
% of total	25	23	26	26

Total second homes: Gwynedd - 6,963

percentage of homes within each parish: Merioneth

Class C: 20.0-29.9%		Class D: 30.0% & over	
Parish	No. of second homes	Parish	No. of second homes
Tywyn	410	Llangelynin	274
Llandanwg	108	Llangower	17
Llandecwyn	18		
Llanfrothen	47		
Talsarnau	53		
Llanaber	47		
Llanenddwyn	109		
Llanfihangel	42		
Mallwyd	54		
Pennal	32		
Talyllyn	81		
	1,001		291

total - 2,069

Table 7.5   Parishes selected as sample

Class A: 0.0-9.9%		Class B: 10.0-19.9%	
Parish	No. of second homes	Parish	No.of second homes
Llaniestyn Rural	1	Llangenedl	75
Rhosybol	8	Penrhoslligwy	12
Llanddaniel Fab	5	Botwynnog	51
Llanbadrig	35	Llanrhychywn	6 from 9
Llanaelhaiarn	46	Llanfair	23
Capel Curig	9		
Maenan	4		
Henryd	3		
Llanymawddwy	2		
Bala	13		
Penrhyndeudraeth	48		
Llanegryn	2 out of 4		
Total	176		167

Table 7.6   Selected parishes by county

Anglesey	Caernarvonshire	Merioneth
Llaniestyn Rural	Llanaelhaiarn	Bala
Rhosybol	Capel Curig	Llanfair
Llanddaniel Fab	Maenan	Penrhyndeudraeth
Llanbadrig	Henryd	Talsarnau
Llangenedl	Botwnnog	Llanegryn
Penrhoslligwy	Llanrhychwyn	Llanymawddwy
Llechylched	Aberdaron	Llangower
Rhoscolyn	Llanbedrog	

by density of second homes

Class C: 20.0-29.9%		Class D: 30.0% & over	
Parish	No. of second homes	Parish	No. of second homes
Llechylched	59	Rhoscolyn	75
Aberdaron	70 from 91	Llanbedrog	91 from 119
Talsarnau	53	Llangower	18
	182		184

Deriving a total from the samples

Very early on in the survey it became apparent that estimates of the density of second homes derived from local authority data varied considerably in their accuracy. This was partly because they had not, in fact, defined the nature of a second home, and partly because estimates of possible second homes from the rating register were inaccurate. We were therefore concerned that deriving a grossing-up percentage for those owners or lessees whose rating demand was sent direct to their second home could well lead to a large error if based on the evidence of a one hundred percent survey of four parishes. We therefore determined to utilize local knowledge in each of the 23 parishes selected for the expenditure sample. At the same time we wished to avoid creating advance publicity and therefore, wherever possible, confined our enquiries to the local policemen and postmasters. Tables 2.1 to 2.3 show a detailed parish-by-parish breakdown of the result of our survey. The results for the county as a whole are summarized in Table 2.4. Table 2.5 shows the total second homes enumerated in the 23 parishes selected. Arranged in their original class densities, i.e. ignoring new densities derived from our investigation, this gave us totals of 125, 55, 97 and 138 for the four classes, these totals comprising 30.12, 13.25, 23.38 and 33.25 percent respectively.

Table 2.6 shows the 23 parishes arranged in the new, i.e. derived, class densities. This gave us totals of 155, 122, 138 and zero for the four classes, these totals comprising 37.35, 29.40, 33.25 and zero percent respectively. A standard statistical test showed that this result would be extremely unlikely to be caused by sampling error.

Our first problem then was to gross up the results of our investigation in order to derive a total of second homes for Gwynedd.

Had the expected number of second homes equalled the observed number of second homes, we should simply have grossed up on the basis of our ten percent sample, deriving in this case a total of 6,963 second homes in Gwynedd. However, since the observed number of second homes differed substantially from the expected number, we considered three possible alternative ways of grossing up.

The first was simply to sum the observed number of second homes in the sample and to divide this by the expected number of second homes in the sample. Multiplying this by the expected total of second homes in Gwynedd would give us:

observed number of second homes in sample   :   415
expected number of second homes in sample   :   709
expected number of second homes in Gwynedd : 6,963 ,

then

$$\frac{\text{observed second homes in sample}}{\text{expected second homes in sample}} \times \text{expected second homes in Gwynedd}$$

$$= \frac{415}{709} \times 6,963$$

$$= 4,076 \text{ second homes.}$$

However, this result is based on the assumption of a constant sampling fraction of a known population, and our constant sampling fraction was of an expected population which differed from the observed population.

We then took the total expected number of second homes in Gwynedd and multiplied this by the sum of the fractions of the observed in the sample over the expected number in the sample for each class density, dividing by the number of class densities. Thus,

$$6{,}963 \; \times \; \frac{\frac{125}{176} + \frac{55}{167} + \frac{97}{182} + \frac{138}{184}}{4} \; = \; 6{,}963 \; \times \; \frac{2.3225355}{4}$$

$$= \; 6{,}963 \; \times \; 0.5806338$$

$$= \; 4{,}043 \text{ second homes.}$$

This, in turn, was based on an erroneous assumption, i.e. that the original densities had been correctly classified. We therefore determined to take ·the number of observed second homes in the original classes, multiply this by the number of dwellings in the class interval, and divide by the number of dwellings in the class in the sample. This has the advantage of re-weighting the results in the sample proportions of the original estimates.

From Table 2.5 the number of second homes observed in each class density is 125, 55, 97, 138 respectively. Then

$$\frac{\text{number of observed second homes} \; \times \; \text{dwellings in each class}}{\text{dwellings in each class in sample}}$$

$$= \; 1{,}726 \; + \; 606 \; + \; 919 \; + \; 1{,}135$$

$$= \; 4{,}386 \text{ second homes.}$$

We examined our non-respondents in the sample for those variables which were available to us, namely type of property, form of property, age of property, garden size of property, location of property, incidence by parish, rateable value, and area of main home, in order to investigate the possibility of systematic bias in the non-response element. We observed no significant differences between respondents and non-respondents based on the above variables.

It will be recalled that we also intended undertaking separate surveys of chalets, caravans and new developments. In the case of caravans we discovered that those caravans which could be used all year were, in fact, occupied all year round, and that the standard response to investigation was that it was a permanent home; alternatively, in the case where it could be used for a part of the year, the response was 'caravans aren't second homes anyway'. Thus this survey was abandoned.

The survey of chalets was hampered by the lack of a uniform defin-ition between local authorities as to what constituted 'a chalet'. At the one pole we have the log-built two- or three-bedroomed cabin with a designed life of more than 25 years and at the other a large caravan. Some sites are freehold, whilst the majority are leased on a year-to-year basis. Eventually we decided that a chalet was a dwelling built of materials other than brick or stone, which possessed neither wheels nor a frame designed to

accept wheels or lifting.   That is, we did not rule out the possibility of
mobility, but we considered that ready mobility was more likely to apply to
caravans than to chalets.

        Investigating the lists of chalets supplied by the local authorities,
we had to establish type of ownership, since a large number of chalets are
owned by a few firms and let on a week-to-week basis.   Further, in order to
comply with our definition, they were not to be subject to a seasonal
licence.   Investigation showed that of the 157 chalets that satisfied our
ownership criterion, only 18 satisfied our availability criterion.   We
established that occupancy levels and income were not dissimilar from that
occupancy level and income manifested by owners of chalets which satisfied
the ownership but not the availability criterion.   We therefore determined
that, rather than abandon our chalet survey, we should conduct a random
sample of chalet owners to establish whether they differed significantly
from owners of 'traditional' second homes.   Our sample was a 20% random
sample survey.

        Our survey of new development houses was finally confined to those
sites where the complexes were obviously designed to cater either for a
particular activity or, alternatively, specifically for second home accommodation.

The derivation of the expenditure figures

        This section describes the methodology used in order to derive the
total expenditure and the expenditure pattern for second home owners and
their nuclear families within Gwynedd for the year 1 August 1973 to 31 July
1974.   The expenditure pattern of second home owners was derived from the
questionnaire shown in Appendix II.

        In our total expenditure figure we have ignored use of second homes
by persons other than the nuclear families of the owners, since this
strictly becomes use of holiday cottages by tourists, and as such is
included in the total expenditure figure for tourism in Gwynedd, as derived
by Archer, Shea and de Vane.[1]   However, it must be borne in mind that
second homes do provide a measure of tourist accommodation, as may be seen
from Table 3.15.

        Similarly we have ignored the expenditure by second home owners on
the construction and alteration of their properties, since these are
strictly historic costs and do not provide any ongoing current benefit in
terms of expenditure.   It is well to remember that second home owners
have spent an average of £970 per property on construction and alteration,
generally in the first two years of ownership.   Current expenditure on
maintenance has been included in the expenditure patterns of second home
owners.

        Where the term 'traditional' has been used in this chapter, it
refers to the present second home structure in Gwynedd, which mainly
comprises old cottages and houses.   Data derived separately for old
cottages and houses would be so similar as to present an unnecessary encumbrance.   It should also be remembered that chalets in the main do not
qualify for inclusion as second homes according to our definition, and are
included for comparison purposes only.

Total expenditure by a second home owner may be thought of as his average expenditure per day on a variety of categories multiplied by the number of days he occupies his property, added to his expenditure on local labour and rate payments.   Thus for all second home owners we have

Total expenditure = *[*(mean expenditure × occupancy rate)

+ mean expenditure on local labour

+ mean rate payment*]* × number of second
homes.

The data to fit this equation are as follows.   From Table 3.14 the mean occupancy rate by owners of traditional second homes is 81.641 nights. Table 4.1 shows that this type of second home owner spends an average of 557.824 pence per day while resident at his second home.   The mean rate payment by traditional second home owners is £53.637, and their average expenditure on local labour is £40.865.   The number of second homes in the traditional category is 4,386.   Then from the above equation

Total expenditure = *[*(557.824 × 81.641) + (40.865) + (53.637)*]*

× 4,386

= £2,413,310.

The same exercise performed for new developments and chalets (bearing in mind the proviso of Chapter 3) gives for new developments

Total expenditure = £114,230

and for chalets

Total expenditure = £45,757.

References

1. B. H. Archer, S. Shea and R. de Vane, *Tourism in Gwynedd: an Economic Study*, Wales Tourist Board, 1974.

CHAPTER EIGHT

THE MODEL

The model used to derive the second home multipliers is an input-output model of Gwynedd adapted from Roland Artle's 'metropolitan' model[1] of the form

$$X - AX - C_{30}(I - A) B_{30}X - \cdots - C_{47}(I - A) B_{47}X = Y \qquad (8.1)$$

X is the vector of total output and is defined as

$$X = \begin{bmatrix} x_1 \\ x_2 \\ \vdots \\ x_{29} \end{bmatrix}$$

where, for example, x_1 is the total output of row 1, x_2 is the total output of row 2, etc.

$$A = \begin{bmatrix} a_{11} & a_{12} & \cdots\cdots\cdots & a_{1n} \\ a_{21} & a_{22} & \cdots\cdots\cdots & a_{2n} \\ \vdots & \vdots & & \vdots \\ a_{n1} & a_{n2} & \cdots\cdots\cdots & a_{nn} \end{bmatrix}$$

where, for example, a_{11} is the coefficient of the sales by row 1 to column 1, i.e. the value of these sales divided by x_1, the total input of column 1

$$C_h = \begin{bmatrix} r_{1h} & r_{1h} & \cdots\cdots\cdots & r_{1h} \\ r_{2h} & r_{2h} & \cdots\cdots\cdots & r_{2h} \\ \vdots & \vdots & & \vdots \\ r_{nh} & r_{nh} & \cdots\cdots\cdots & r_{nh} \end{bmatrix}$$

where $h = 30$ to 47, and C_h is one of a series of 18 matrices, each representing the consumption pattern of a particular household category. 18 different socio-economic types of household were identified and, in consequence, it was possible to assess the induced effects of the re-spending of additional income separately for each household type.

$$
B_h = \begin{bmatrix}
B_{h1} & 0 & \cdots\cdots & 0 \\
0 & B_{h2} & \cdots\cdots & 0 \\
\vdots & \vdots & & \vdots \\
0 & 0 & \cdots\cdots & B_{hn}
\end{bmatrix}
$$

where $h = 30$ to 47 and B_h represents one of a series of 18 matrices, each representing the income characteristics of the 18 socio-economic categories above.

Y is the vector of export demand and is defined as

$$
Y = \begin{bmatrix}
y_1 \\
y_2 \\
\vdots \\
y_{29}
\end{bmatrix}
$$

I is the identity matrix shown by

$$
I = \begin{bmatrix}
1 & 0 & \cdots\cdots & 0 \\
0 & 1 & \cdots\cdots & 0 \\
\vdots & \vdots & & \vdots \\
0 & 0 & \cdots\cdots & 1
\end{bmatrix}
$$

We must first factor X and sum the consumption demand to give

$$
\left[I - A - \sum_{h=29}^{47} C_h \, (I - A) \, B_h \right] X = Y \tag{8.2}
$$

Factoring out $(I - A)$ gives

$$
\left[I - \sum_{h=29}^{47} C_h \, (I - A) \, B_h \, (I - A)^{-1} \right] (I - A) \, X = Y \tag{8.3}
$$

Solving for X gives

$$X = (I - A)^{-1} \left[I - \sum_{h=29}^{47} C_h (I - A) B_h (I - A)^{-1} \right]^{-1} Y \qquad (8.4)$$

The working of the model can best be explained from equation 8.1 above. From the total output, X, is subtracted first the intermediate demand, AX, then the Gwynedd householders' final demand,

$$C_{30} (I - A) B_{30}X - \cdots - C_{47} (I - A) B_{47}X,$$

to leave 'export' sales (sales outside Gwynedd), Y.

The manipulations described in equations 8.2, 8.3 and 8.4 above are designed to produce a model which relates export sales functionally to both transactions and incomes in the regional economy. Thus the effect of an increase in second home spending in any part of the Y vector can be traced through each sector of the regional economy. The method used in this model to relate income earnings to consumer expenditure is unique. An even more rigorous refinement to the model is the allowances which are made for shifts in consumer expenditure patterns. As householders' income levels rise, their consumption patterns change. This affects not only the proportions of income which they spend on each type of good and service, but also where they purchase the items. For example, if, because of an increase in incomes, consumer demand for a good normally purchased within the region falls, the net effect is a *fall* in regional income. Conversely, rises in personal incomes might lead to a proportional switch of consumer spending to goods and services sold within the region with, in consequence, a more than proportional induced rise in regional incomes. The sub-model used for these calculations is given below; it is described in detail in Sadler *et al.*, *Regional Income Multipliers.*[2]

(1) Assume an average income for group X of $\bar{A}$.

(2) Group X contains n incomes between the limits A_1 and A_2.

(3) The proportion of total income in X spent on commodity i is α_i.

Thus the total expenditure by group X on i is $\bar{A}n\alpha_1$.

(4) Suppose all incomes in group X are multiplied by $\delta (\delta > 1)$.

Average income of the individuals concerned is now $\bar{A}\delta$, and the limits of their income are now $A_1\delta$ to $A_2\delta$. As $\delta > 1$, some of these incomes now fall outside the former upper limit, A_2. Suppose now that in the group next above X (call it Y) the average proportion spent on i is βi, and that new entrants into this group alter their spending patterns to conform to those within the group. A reasonable approximation of the income which would be transferred to Y is

$$\bar{A}n\delta \frac{A_2\delta - A_2}{A_2\delta - A_1\delta},$$

while that remaining in group X would be

$$\bar{A}n\delta - \bar{A}n\delta \frac{A_2\delta - A_2}{A_2\delta - A_1\delta}$$

(5)   The proportion of each of these spent on i would be βi and αi respectively, and the question is whether the total expenditure on i is greater or less than it was before.

(6)   If we sum the two totals of expenditure and divide this by the old expenditure, the result will be $\gtrless 1$ according to whether more, the same, or less is spent on i than before, thus

$$\frac{\beta_i \left\{ \bar{A}n\delta \dfrac{A_2\delta - A_2}{A_2\delta - A_1\delta} \right\} + \alpha_i \left\{ \bar{A}n\delta - \bar{A}n\delta \dfrac{A_2\delta - A_2}{A_2\delta - A_1\delta} \right\}}{\alpha_i \bar{A}n}$$

This can be simplified to

$$\frac{\beta_i}{\alpha_i} \delta \frac{A_2\delta - A_2}{A_2\delta - A_1\delta} + \delta - \delta \frac{A_2\delta - A_2}{A_2\delta - A_1\delta}$$

and further to

$$\delta + \frac{A_2(\delta-1)}{A_2 - A_1} \left\{ \frac{\beta_i}{\alpha_i} - 1 \right\}.$$

(7)   Whether more or less is spent on commodity i now depends upon the size of the increase as represented by the multiplier δ, and the value of the proportion $\dfrac{\beta_i}{\alpha_i}$.

$\dfrac{A_2(\delta-1)}{A_2 - A_1}$ is always positive, but if $\dfrac{\beta_i}{\alpha_i}$ is less than 1, $\dfrac{\beta_i}{\alpha_i} -1$ will be negative, so that the change in the quantity of i demanded will be less than δ.   If the value of this negative component exceeds $\delta-1$, the total amount demanded will be less than before the change.

References

1.   R. Artle, 'On some methods and problems in the study of metropolitan economics', *Regional Science Association Papers*, Vol.8, Hague Congress, 1961, pp. 71-87.

2.   P. G. Sadler, B. H. Archer and C. B. Owen, *Regional Income Multipliers*, Bangor Occasional Papers in Economics, No.1, University of Wales Press, 1973.

APPENDIX I

DATA SOURCES FOR THE MODEL

APPENDIX I

DATA SOURCES FOR THE MODEL

General approach

As in the case of the earlier Anglesey study, a list of establishments in Gwynedd was compiled from the following sources:

(1) general rates books of the local councils

(2) employers registers issued by the Department of Employment for each employment exchange area (these registers give only firms with five or more employees)

(3) records of the Consumer Protection Departments of the county councils

(4) Census of Distribution 1966 for the three counties concerned

(5) some preliminary tables of the Census of Distribution 1971.

The list had to be amended during the survey to allow for unrecorded changes in the number and type of establishments.

The information needed for the industry × industry transactions matrix was obtained in three main ways.

(1) In the case of manufacturing industries, mining and quarrying establishments and wholesalers, a direct approach was made to each firm. The eventual response rate was approximately 68%.

(2) For many activities, however, notably gas, electricity, forestry etc., information was obtained from the relevant head offices situated outside the Gwynedd area.

(3) Data for some sectors, especially retailing and service trades, were obtained on a sample basis.

The 1968 M.L.H. (minimum list headings) classification was followed. In all 29 sectors were used in the input-output table.

Sectors

(1) *Agriculture and forestry*

The data sources used to compile the agricultural sector, the problems encountered and the methods used to overcome these difficulties were exactly the same as in the earlier Anglesey study (see Sadler *et al.*,

82

Regional Income Multipliers, pp. 99-101).

Figures for forestry operations in Gwynedd were provided by the Forestry Commission authorities at Aberystwyth.

(2) *Quarrying*

Direct enquiry yielded usable information on revenue, wages and other costs for 34 of the 50 quarries within Gwynedd. Figures for the remaining 16 quarries were assessed on the basis of (i) their number of employees and (ii) their rateable values in relation to the known figures for the other quarries.

(3) to (6) *Manufacturing*

For the input-output table, firms were grouped into 4 categories corresponding to the following S.I.C. (Standard Industrial Classification) 1968 Orders:

(i)	Engineering	:	Orders VI to XII
(ii)	Textiles	:	Orders XIII to XV
(iii)	Timber	:	Order XVII
(iv)	Others	:	Orders III, V, XVI, XVIII and XIX.

Full information was obtained by direct enquiry from 33 major firms out of a total of 43. Usable data were obtained about the remaining 10 firms.

(7) *Construction*

Information was obtained by direct enquiry from the major construction firms within Gwynedd, but difficulties arose in obtaining usable data about the operations of small establishments. The problems encountered and the methods used to overcome them were the same as in the earlier Anglesey study (see Sadler *et al.*, *Regional Income Multipliers*, pp. 101-2).

(8) *Gas*

Full information about this sector was provided by the Wales Gas Board (Economics Division) in Cardiff.

(9) *Electricity*

Information about the sales of electricity and appliances in Gwynedd was provided by the M.A.N.W.E.B. office in Chester. The M.A.N.W.E.B. figures gave a breakdown of sales into six main sectors, and these were further apportioned between sectors by using empirical evidence obtained from the survey of establishments.

The C.E.G.B. office in Manchester provided further information about electricity generation and transmission on a station-by-station basis. For the purposes of the input-output table, the generated power was treated, where relevant, as an export.

(10) *Water*

The various water boards provided full information about their revenue, cost and employment statistics.

(11) *Rail transport*

Information was obtained from the British Rail office at Stoke-on-Trent, supplemented by empirical data gathered from business establishments during the survey.

(12) *Road transport*

With the exception of one large operator, road transport is mainly controlled by a number of small and medium sized firms, some of them working on a part-time basis. The firms involved cover a wide range of activities, including coach, minibus, taxi-cab and car-hire, cartage and haulage, including the haulage of sand, gravel and construction materials. Less than half of the smaller establishments co-operated in providing information and the resultant data were grossed up on the basis of the respective sizes of the firms and from information obtained from those other sectors of the economy which use road transport. Employment figures were provided by the Department of Employment.

(13) *Ports*

Information for this sector was obtained from British Rail and from local employment records, supplemented by data obtained from those firms which use the port facilities.

(14) *Postal and telecommunications*

Detailed data were obtained by direct enquiry from (a) Wales and the Marches Telecommunications Board in Cardiff and (b) Wales and the Marches Postal Board in Cardiff.

(15) *Insurance, banking and finance*

Information for this sector was based on (a) a survey of some of the branch establishments, (b) information provided by one of the principal banks and (c) Department of Employment employment records. This was supplemented by empirical data obtained from firms in other sectors.

(16) *Education*

This sector, unlike the previous Anglesey study, excludes local authority educational institutions and administration and is therefore concerned with private educational bodies and with the University College of North Wales. Public sector education was included within the local government sector.

(17) to (22) *Garages; hotels, public houses, caravan sites, etc.; food shops; non-food shops; wholesalers; other services*

The methods used to obtain data for these sectors were identical with those employed in the earlier Anglesey study. Particular care was taken to include a large sample of hotels and other tourist accommodation units within the empirical survey.

The total numbers of retail establishments etc. in Gwynedd was obtained by reference to the following sources:

(1)   1966 County Census Reports
(2)   County Medical Officers' Reports for the three counties
(3)   general rates books
(4)   Census of Distribution, 1971
(5)   Abstracts of Statistics of the county councils
(6)   the employment records of the Department of Employment.

(23) *Professional and scientific*

The number of people in Order XXV, excluding M.L.H. 872 Education, was obtained from the following sources:

(1)   employment records of the Department of Employment
(2)   1966 County Census Reports
(3)   direct enquiry.

Wages and salaries were obtained for some categories, e.g. medical and dental services, from the Welsh Office and the relevant hospital boards. For others, where accurate salary data were unavailable, the numbers in each category were multiplied by the average earnings of the occupation concerned.

(24) *Local government*

Each local authority is required by law to submit annually to the Department of the Environment a complete statement of its financial activities on both current and capital account. These statements were used to obtain total inputs and outputs.

A more detailed breakdown of these figures was obtained from the following:

(1)   general rates estimates
(2)   Abstracts of Statistics of the various local authorities
(3)   contracts books
(4)   invoices
(5)   direct enquiry.

Considerable care had to be taken, particularly in the cases of the Housing Revenue Account, of all capital transactions and of transfers to county authorities, to avoid double counting.

(25) *National government*

Full information was obtained by direct enquiry at the relevant local offices.

(26) *Defence establishments*

Detailed information was provided by the Ministry of Defence in London about the cost structure of the various military establishments in Gwynedd. The total output of these establishments was shown as equal to the sum of the various inputs, excluding the value of aircraft, vehicles, fuel, etc. brought into Gwynedd.

Other information

The methodology used to derive the values of exports, imports, Gwynedd final demand, local earned and unearned incomes, taxation and other payments and to compile the consumption and income matrices followed the same procedures as for the earlier Anglesey study (details of these can be found in Sadler et al., *Regional Income Multipliers*, pp.107-109).

The sectoral multipliers obtained are shown in Table A1.

Table A.1   Sectoral multipliers in Gwynedd, 1973

	Direct income	Direct, indirect & induced income	'Orthodox' income multiplier	'Unorthodox' income multiplier	Sales multiplier
	(1)	(2)	(3)	(4)	(5)
1. Agriculture	0.4756	0.6941	1.46	0.69	1.80
2. Quarrying	0.5573	0.7414	1.33	0.74	1.70
3. Engineering	0.1917	0.2397	1.25	0.24	1.21
4. Textiles	0.1674	0.2012	1.20	0.20	1.14
5. Timber	0.1595	0.2145	1.35	0.21	1.24
6. Other manufacturing	0.1843	0.2991	1.62	0.30	1.38
7. Construction	0.3486	0.5569	1.60	0.56	1.73
8. Gas	0.1393	0.1823	1.32	0.35	1.38
9. Electricity	0.1393	0.1823	1.31	0.18	1.19
10. Water	0.3189	0.4231	1.33	0.42	1.40
11. Rail transport	0.6937	0.8711	1.26	0.87	1.75
12. Road transport	0.4988	0.6434	1.29	0.64	1.60
13. Ports	0.9879	1.2124	1.23	1.21	1.97
14. Postal and telecommunications	0.3328	0.3966	1.19	0.40	1.27
15. Insurance, banking and finance	0.5039	0.6475	1.28	0.65	1.58
16. Education	0.6536	0.7893	1.21	0.79	1.56
17. Garage trade	0.1061	0.1334	1.26	0.13	1.12
18. Hotels etc.	0.2502	0.3594	1.44	0.36	1.46
19. Food shops	0.1426	0.2558	1.79	0.26	1.57
20. Non-food shops	0.2097	0.2860	1.36	0.29	1.37
21. Wholesalers	0.1111	0.2877	2.59	0.29	1.51
22. Other services	0.6108	0.7469	1.22	0.75	1.52
23. Professional and scientific	0.8782	1.0827	1.23	1.08	1.81
24. Local government	0.3734	0.5052	1.35	0.51	1.54
25. National government	0.3682	0.4493	1.22	0.45	1.32
26. Defence	0.3958	0.5051	1.27	0.51	1.47
27. Exogenous income	1.1004	1.1209	1.02	1.12	1.50

APPENDIX II

QUESTIONNAIRES USED IN THE STUDY

TRADITIONAL CONSTRUCTION

PLEASE TICK APPROPRIATE BOX

TYPE OF PROPERTY

House
Bungalow
Cottage
Flat

(1)

FORM OF PROPERTY

Detached
Semi-detached
Terraced
Other

(2)

AGE OF PROPERTY

0 - 10 yrs.
11 - 30 yrs.
31 - 75 yrs.
Over 75 yrs.

(3)

GARDEN SIZE OF PROPERTY

No garden
Less than ¼ acre
¼ - 1 acre
1 - 5 acres
6 - 10 acres
Over 10 acres

(4)

LOCATION OF PROPERTY

Isolated
Hamlet
Village
Town

(5)

PARISH

(6)

87

1. Do you own, rent or lease from someone else any
   residential property, other than your permanent home?

   Own

   Lease or rent   (7)

   Neither

   > If answer is NEITHER terminate interview

2. (a) Is this property available, if required, for   Yes
       your exclusive use over a 12-month period?   No

   (b) Do you consider this property to be your   Yes   (8)
       second home?   No

   > If answer is NO terminate interview

3. When did you purchase/rent/acquire the property?   `1 9`   (9)   `1 9`

   > If purchased go to 4
   > If rented go to 6

4. Did you purchase the property from:

   a local owner?

   a second home owner?

   a distant owner?   (10)

   an estate agent?

   was it purpose-built?

5. Would you mind telling me the purchase price?

   £   (11)

   Was it a cash purchase?   Yes
                  No   (12)

   > Go to 7

6. Would you mind telling me the annual rent?

   Less than £50

   £51 - 150

   £151 - 300

   £301 - 450

   £451 - 600   (13)

   £601 - 750

   £751 plus (give figure:

   £ ....)

88

7.(a) How many bed spaces are there in the property?

1
2
3
4
5
6
7
8

(14)

(b) How many bedrooms are there?

(15)

8. How many people usually make up your visiting group?

1
2
3
4
5
6
7
8

(16)

9. When you acquired it, was your property ...

an old property in need of modernization?
a modernized property?
a new property?

(17)

10. If the final costs of these properties were equal, and you had a choice, would you prefer ...

an old property in need of modernization?
a modernized old property?
a new property?
no preference

(18)

11. Please indicate the approximate number of nights you and your family have spent in the property during the last year

1973: August
September
October
Nov./Dec.
1974: Jan./Feb.
March
April
May
June
July

(19)
(20)
(21)
(22)
(23)
(24)
(25)
(26)
(27)
(28)

12. Do you lend or hire the property during the year: Yes
No

(29)

| If YES go to 13; if NO go to 15 |

13. Please indicate the approximate number of nights the property was used by people other than you or your visitor group during last year

1973: August
September
October
Nov./Dec.
1974: Jan./Feb.
March
April
May
June
July

(30)
(31)
(32)
(33)
(34)
(35)
(36)
(37)
(38)
(39)

14. If you received a payment for this, would you mind giving me an idea of how much last year?

£   (40)

15. Which of these alterations and repairs have you undertaken since acquiring the property?

Alterations	*Expenditure (£)*	
Renew/replaster walls		(41)
Connect/re-wire electricity		(42)
Renew floors		(43)
Installed flush toilet		(44)
Installed bath		(45)
Installed septic tank		(46)
Re-roofed		(47)
Total		

16. If you received a grant towards the cost from the Local Authority, would you please tell me how much?

£   (48)

17. Please indicate the amount spent by your visitor group per *DAY* on the following categories on a typical visit

£   p

Food shops		(49)
Souvenirs		(50)
Non-food shops		(51)
Pub/hotel/cafe		(52)
Garage		(53)
Electricity		(54)
Gas Board		(55)
Rail transport		(56)
Road transport		(57)
Other services		(58)
Total		

18. How much, if any, do you spend *PER ANNUM* on local labour, e.g. gardener?

£   p.a.   (59)

19. What made you decide to acquire a second home? Of these reasons which *ONE* did you consider the most important?

A wish to sub-let it	(60)
As a capital investment	(61)
For eventual retirement	(62)
For holiday/weekend accommodation	(63)
Because you wanted to be near friends/relatives	(64)
Other (please specify)........................	(65)
....	

90

20. Have you now decided (when the times comes) to retire to:

        Your second home
        Somewhere else within the county
        Elsewhere   (66) ☐
  OR: Not yet decided
        same use
Which year do you expect to retire?   (67) ☐☐☐☐

21. How many people in your immediate family are
in the following categories?

	1) under 5	number		(68) ☐
	2) 5 - 14	"		(69) ☐
Enter a number in	3) 15 - 19	"		(70) ☐
the appropriate box	4) 20 - 29	"		(71) ☐
	5) 30 - 49	"		(72) ☐
	6) 50 - 65	"		(73) ☐
	7) over 65	"		(74) ☐

22. Are you (or your husband):   employed?
                          self-employed?
                          unemployed?   (75) ☐
                          retired?

23. What kind of work do you (or your husband) do?

	factory	1
	transport	2
MANUAL	building	3
	farm	4
Show Card A	other manual	5
	professional	6
NON-MANUAL	director, proprietor, manager	7
	shop, personal service	8
	office and all others	9

(76) ☐

24. What was the family income when you first became
a second home owner?

	less than £3,000 per annum	1
	£3,001 - 3,500 " "	2
	£3,501 - 4,000 " "	3
Show Card B	£4,001 - 4,500 " "	4
	£4,501 - 5,000 " "	5
	£5,001 - 5,500 " "	6
	£5,501 - 6,000 " "	7
	£6,001 plus " "	8

(77) ☐

25. What is the family income now?

        less than £3,000 " "   1
        £3,001 - 3,500   2
        £3,501 - 4,000   3
        £4,001 - 4,500   4   (78) ☐
        £4,501 - 5,000   5
        £5,001 - 5,500   6
        £5,501 - 6,000   7
        £6,001 plus   8

91

26. When did you finish your full-time education?

At or below 15 years?
Between 15 and 20 years?
After degree or other qualification at a
    university of a similar place of higher
    education?

| Thank you very much for your co-operation |

PLEASE TICK APPROPRIATE BOX

For Office use only

GARDEN SIZE OF PROPERTY

No garden
Less than ¼ acre
¼ - 1 acre
1 - 5 acres
6 - 10 acres
over 10 acres

85

NUMBER OF RESIDENTIAL
CARAVANS ON SITE

2 - 5
6 - 10
11 - 15
16 - 20
21 - 50
51 - 100
Over 101

86

LOCATION OF CARAVAN

Isolated
Hamlet
Village
Town

87

PARISH

88

93

1. Do you own, rent or lease from someone else any
   residential property (including a caravan other than
   your permanent home?

   Own
   Lease or rent   89 ☐
   Neither

   | If answer is NEITHER terminate interview |

2. (a) Is this caravan available, if required, for   Yes
       your exclusive use over a 12-month period?   No
                                                                 90 ☐
   (b) Do you consider this caravan to be your   Yes
       second home?   No

   | If answer is No terminate interview |

3. When did you purchase/rent/acquire the caravan?   ⬚⬚⬚⬚ 91 ⬚⬚⬚⬚⬚

   | If purchased go to 4; if rented go to 6 |

4. Did you purchase the caravan from: A local owner?
                                        A second home owner?
                                        A distant owner?   92 ☐
                                        A dealer?

5. Would you mind telling me the purchase price? £ ⬚⬚⬚⬚⬚ 93 ⬚⬚⬚⬚⬚

   Was it a cash purchase?   Yes   94 ☐
                                                    No

   | Go to 7 |

6. Would you mind telling me the annual rent?

                              Less than £50
                               £51 - 150
                               £151 - 300
                               £301 - 450   95 ⬚⬚⬚⬚⬚
                               £451 - 600
                               £601 - 750.
                               £751 plus
                              (give figure) £.....

7. (a) Do you pay a separate site rent?   Yes   96 ☐
                                                     No

   (b) Would you mind telling me how much?   £   p.a. 97 ⬚⬚⬚

   | If answer is NO go to 8 |

94

8. How many bed spaces are there in the caravan?

1
2
3
4
5
6
7
8

98 ☐

9. How many people usually make up your visiting group?

1.
2
3
4
5
6
7
8

99 ☐

10. If the final costs of these properties were equal, and you had a choice, would you prefer:

an old property in need of modernization?
a modernized old property?
a new property?
a caravan?
no preference?

100 ☐

11. Please indicate the approximate number of nights you and your family have spent in the caravan during the last year

1973:	August	101
	September	102
	October	103
	Nov./Dec.	104
1974:	Jan./Feb.	105
	March	106
	April	107
	May	108
	June	109
	July	110

12. Do you lend or hire the caravan during the year?   Yes   No

111, ☐

> If YES go to 13; if NO go to 15

13. Please indicate the approximate number of nights the caravan was used by people other than you or your visitor group during last year:

1973:	August	112
	September	113
	October	114
	Nov./Dec.	115
1974:	Jan./Feb.	116
	March	117
	April	118
	May	119
	June	120
	July	121

95

14. If you received payment for this, would you mind giving me an idea of how much last year? £ ☐☐☐☐ 122 ☐☐☐☐

15. Please indicate the amount spent by your visitor group *PER DAY* on the following categories on a typical visit

	£	p	
Food shops			123
Souvenirs			124
Non-food shops			125
Pub/hotel/cafe			126
Garage			127
Electricity			128
Gas Board			129
Rail transport			130
Road transport			131
Other services			132
Total			

16. How much, if any, do you spend *PER ANNUM* on local labour, e.g. gardener? £ ☐☐☐☐ p.a. 133 ☐☐☐

17. What made you decide to acquire a second home? Of these reasons which *ONE* did you consider most important?

a wish to sub-let it 134
as a capital investment 135
for eventual retirement 136
for holiday/weekend accommodation 137
because you wanted to be near friends/relatives 138
other (please specify) 139

....

18. Have you now decided (when the time comes) to retire to:

your second home
somewhere else within the county 140
elsewhere
OR: not yet decided
same use
Which year do you expect to retire? ☐☐☐☐ 141 ☐☐☐☐

19. How many people in your immediate family are in the following categories?

		number	
1) under 5	number		142
2) 5 - 14	"		143
3) 15 - 19	"		144
4) 20 - 29	"		145
5) 30 - 49	"		146
6) 50 - 65	"		147
7) over 65	"		148

Enter a number in the appropriate box

96

20. Are you (or your husband):

employed?
self-employed?
unemployed?
retired?

21. What kind of work do you (or your husband) do?

MANUAL	factory	1
	transport	2
	building	3
	farm	4
	other manual	5

Show Card A

NON-MANUAL	professional	6
	director, proprietor, manager	7
	shop, personal service	8
	office and all others	9

150

22. What was the family income when you first became a second home owner?

less than £3,000 per annum			1
£3,001 - 3,500	"	"	2
£3,501 - 4,000	"	"	3
£4,001 - 4,500	"	"	4
£4,501 - 5,000	"	"	5
£5,001 - 5,500	"	"	6
£5,501 - 6,000	"	"	7
£6,001 plus	"	"	8

Show Card B

151

23. What is the family income now?

less than £3,000	"	"	1
£3,001 - 3,500	"	"	2
£3,501 - 4,000	"	"	3
£4,001 - 4,500	"	"	4
£4,501 - 5,000	"	"	5
£5,001 - 5,500	"	"	6
£5,501 - 6,000	"	"	7
£6,001 plus	"	"	8

152

24. When did you finish your full-time education?

at or below 15 years?
between 15 and 20 years?
after degree or other qualification at
   a university or a similar place of
   higher education?

153

Thank you very much for your co-operation

154

155

PLEASE TICK APPROPRIATE BOX

For Office use only

GARDEN SIZE OF PROPERTY   No garden
                             Less than ¼ acre
                             ¼ - 1 acre   160
                             1 - 5 acres
                             6 - 10 acres
                             over 10 acres

NUMBER OF RESIDENTIAL
CHALETS ON SITE   2 - 5
                             6 - 10
                             11 - 15
                             16 - 20   161
                             21 - 50
                             51 - 100
                             Over 101

LOCATION OF CHALET   Isolated
                             Hamlet
                             Village   162
                             Town

PARISH   163

1. Do you own, rent or lease from someone else any
    residential property (including a chalet) other than
    your permanent home?

                                    Own
                                    Lease or rent   164 ☐
                                    Neither

    ┌───┐
    │ If answer is NEITHER terminate interview   │
    └───┘

2. (a) Is this chalet available, if required, for   Yes
        your exclusive use over a 12-month period?   No
                                                              165 ☐
    (b) Do you consider this chalet to be your   Yes
        second home?   No

    ┌───┐
    │ If answer is No terminate interview   │
    └───┘

3. When did you purchase/rent/acquire the chalet?   ☐☐☐   166 ☐☐☐☐☐

    ┌───┐
    │ If purchased go to 4; if rented go to 6   │
    └───┘

4. Did you purchase the chalet from: A local owner?
                                        A second home owner?
                                        A distant owner?   167 ☐
                                        A dealer?

5. Would you mind telling me the purchase price? £ ☐☐☐☐☐   168 ☐☐☐☐☐

    Was it a cash purchase?   Yes
                                                      No   169 ☐

    ┌──────────────┐
    │ Go to 7   │
    └──────────────┘

6. Would you mind telling me the annual rent?

                              Less than £50
                               £51 - 150
                              £151 - 300
                              £301 - 450   170 ☐☐☐☐
                              £451 - 600
                              £601 - 750
                              £751 plus
                              (give figure) £.....

7. (a) Do you pay a separate site rent?   Yes
                                                   No   171 ☐

    (b) Would you mind telling me how much?   £   p.a. 172 ☐☐☐

    ┌───┐
    │ If answer is NO go to 8   │
    └───┘

99

8. How many bed spaces are there in the chalet?

1
2
3
4
5
6
7
8

173.

9. How many people usually make up your visiting group?

1
2
3
4
5
6
7
8

174

10. If the final costs of these properties were equal, and you had a choice, would you prefer:

an old property in need of modernization?
a modernized old property?
a new property?
a chalet?
no preference?

175

11. Please indicate the approximate number of nights you and your family have spent in the chalet during the last year

1973:	August	176
	September	177
	October	178
	Nov./Dec.	179
1974:	Jan./Feb.	180
	March	181
	April	182
	May	183
	June	184
	July	185

12. Do you lend or hire the chalet during the year?   Yes   No   186

If YES go to 13; if NO go to 15

13. Please indicate the approximate number of nights the chalet was used by people other than you or your visitor group during last year:

1973:	August	187
	September	188
	October	189
	Nov./Dec.	190
1974:	Jan./Feb.	191
	March	192
	April	193
	May	194
	June	195
	July	196

100

14. If you received payment for this, would you mind
giving me an idea of how much last year? £ [ ][ ][ ] 197 [ ][ ][ ][ ]

15. Please indicate the amount spent by your visitor group
PER DAY on the following categories on a typical visit

	£	p	
Food shops			198
Souvenirs			199
Non-food shops			200
Pub/hotel/cafe			201
Garage			202
Electricity			203
Gas Board			204
Rail transport			205
Road transport			206
Other services			207
Total			

16. How much, if any, do you spend *PER ANNUM*
on local labour, e.g. gardener? £ [ ][ ][ ] p.a. 208 [ ][ ][ ][ ]

17. What made you decide to acquire a second home? Of these
reasons which *ONE* did you consider most important?

a wish to sub-let it [ ] 209
as a capital investment [ ] 210
for eventual retirement [ ] 211
for holiday/weekend accommodation [ ] 212
because you wanted to be near friends/relatives [ ] 213
other (please specify) .... [ ] 214

....

18. Have you now decided (when the time comes) to retire to:

your second home
somewhere else within the county
elsewhere . 215 [ ]
OR: not yet decided
same use

Which year do you expect to retire? [ ][ ][ ][ ] 216 [ ][ ][ ][ ]

19. How many people in your immediate family are in the
following categories?

1) under 5	number	[ ]	217	[ ]
2) 5 - 14	"	[ ]	218	[ ]
3 15 - 19	"	[ ]	219	[ ]
4) 20 - 29	"	[ ]	220	[ ]
5) 30 - 49	"	[ ]	221	[ ]
6) 50 - 65	"	[ ]	222	[ ]
7) over 65	"	[ ]	223	[ ]

Enter a number in the
appropriate box

101

20. Are you (or your husband):   employed?
                                    self-employed?
                                    unemployed?
                                    retired?

224

21. What kind of work do you (or your husband) do?

MANUAL	factory	1
	transport	2
	building	3
	farm	4
	other manual	5

Show Card A

225

NON-MANUAL	professional	6
	director, proprietor, manager	7
	shop, personal service	8
	office and all others	9

22. What was the family income when you first became a
    second home owner?

less than £3,000 per annum		1
£3,001 - 3,500 " "		2
£3,501 - 4,000 " "		3
£4,001 - 4,500 " "		4
£4,501 - 5,000 " "		5
£5,001 - 5,500 " "		6
£5,501 - 6,000 " "		7
£6,001 plus " "		8

Show Card B

226

23. What is the family income now?

less than £3,000 " "		1
£3,001 - 3,500 " "		2
£3,501 - 4,000 " "		3
£4,001 - 4,500 " "		4
£4,501 - 5,000 " "		5
£5,001 - 5,500 " "		6
£5,501 - 6,000 " "		7
£6,001 plus " "		8

227

24. When did you finish your full-time education?

at or below 15 years?
between 15 and 20 years?
after degree or other qualification at
    a university or a similar place of
    higher education?

228

Thank you very much for your co-operation

229

230

102

N E W   D E V E L O P M E N T S

PLEASE TICK APPROPRIATE BOX

TYPE OF PROPERTY

House
Bungalow
Cottage
Flat

240

FORM OF PROPERTY

Detached
Semi-detached
Terraced
Other

241

AGE OF PROPERTY

0 - 10 yrs.
11 - 30 yrs.
31 - 75 yrs.
over 75 yrs.

242

GARDEN SIZE OF PROPERTY

No garden
less than ¼ acre
¼ - 1 acre
1 - 5 acres
6 - 10 acres
Over 10 acres

243

LOCATION OF PROPERTY

Isolated
Hamlet
Village
Town

244

PARISH

245

1. Do you own, rent or lease from someone else any residential property, other than your permanent home?

Own ☐
Lease or rent ☐
Neither ☐

246 ☐

| If answer is NEITHER terminate interview |

2. (a) Is this property available, if required, for your exclusive use over a 12-month period? Yes ☐ No ☐

(b) Do you consider this property to be your second home? Yes ☐ No ☐

247 ☐

| If answer is NO terminate interview |

3. When did you purchase/rent/acquire the property?

1 9 ☐ ☐

248 1 9 ☐ ☐

| If purchased go to 4
If rented go to 6 |

4. Did you purchase the property from:

a local owner? ☐
a second home owner? ☐
a distant owner? ☐
an estate agent? ☐
was it purpose-built? ☐

249 ☐

5. Would you mind telling me the purchase price?

£ ☐☐☐☐

250 ☐☐☐☐☐

Was it a cash purchase? Yes ☐ No ☐

251 ☐

| Go to 7 |

6. Would you mind telling me the annual rent?

Less than £50 ☐
£51 – 150 ☐
£151 – 300 ☐
£301 – 450 ☐
£451 – 600 ☐
£601 – 750 ☐
£751 plus (give figure) £ .... ☐

252 ☐☐☐☐

7. (a) How many bed spaces are there in the property?

1
2
3
4
5
6
7
8

253 ☐

(b) How many bedrooms are there? ☐

254 ☐

8. How many people usually make up your visiting group?

1
2
3
4
5
6
7
8

255 ☐

9. If the final costs of these properties were equal,
    and you had a choice, would you prefer:

     an old property in need of modernization?
     a modernized old property?
     a new property?
     no preference

256 ☐

10. Please indicate the approximate number of nights you and
    your family have spent in the property during the last year

		257	
1973:	August	257	
	September	258	
	October	259	
	Nov./Dec.	260	
1974:	Jan./Feb.	261	
	March	262	
	April	263	
	May	264	
	June	265	
	July	266	

11. Do you lend or hire the property during the year?   Yes
                                                         No

267 ☐

If YES go to 12; if NO go to 14

12. Please indicate the approximate number of nights the
    property was used by people other than you or your visiting
    group during last year:

1973:	August	268	
	September	269	
	October	270	
	Nov./Dec.	271	
1974:	Jan./Feb.	272	
	March	273	
	April	274	
	May	275	
	June	276	
	July	277	

105

13. If you received a payment for this, would you mind
     giving me an idea of how much last year?

     £ [   ]   278 [| | |]

14. Please indicate the amount spent by your visiting group
     PER DAY on the following categories on a typical visit:

	£	p		
Food shops			279	
Souvenirs			280	
Non-food shops			281	
Pub/hotel/cafe			282	
Garage			283	
Electricity			284	
Gas Board			285	
Rail transport			286	
Road transport			287	
Other services			288	

                    Total

15. How much, if any, do you spend *PER ANNUM*
     on local labour, e.g. gardener?

     £ [   ] p.a.   289 [| |]

16. What made you decide to acquire a second home? Of these
     reasons which *ONE* did you consider the most important?

A wish to sub-let it		290	
As a capital investment		291	
For eventual retirement		292	
For holiday/weekend accommodation		293	
Because you wanted to be near friends/relatives		294	
Other (please specify)		295	

     ....
     ....

17. Have you now decided (when the times comes) to retire to:

Your second home
Somewhere else within the county
Elsewhere
Not yet decided   -
Same use

296 ☐

Which year do you expect to retire?   297 ☐☐☐☐

18. How many people in your immediate family are in the following categories?

Enter a number in the appropriate box	1) under 5	number	298 ☐
	2) 5 - 14	"	299 ☐
	3) 15 - 19	"	300 ☐
	4) 20 - 29	"	301 ☐
	5) 30 - 49	"	302 ☐
	6) 50 - 65	"	303 ☐
	7) over 65	"	304 ☐

19. Are you (or your husband):   employed?
self-employed?
unemployed?   305 ☐
retired?

20. What kind of work do you (or your husband) do?

MANUAL

Show Card A

factory   1
transport   2
building   3
farm   4
other manual   5

306 ☐

NON-MANUAL

professional   6
director, proprietor, manager   7
shop, personal service   8
office and all others   9

21. What was the family income when you first became a second home owner?

Show Card B

less than £3,000 per annum   1
£3,001 - 3,500   "   "   2
£3,501 - 4,000   "   "   3
£4,001 - 4,500   "   "   4
£4,501 - 5,000   "   "   5
£5,001 - 5,500   "   "   6
£5,501 - 6,000   "   "   7
£6,001 plus   "   "   8

307 ☐

22. What is the family income now?

less than £3,000   "   "   1
£3,001 - 3,500   2
£3,501 - 4,000   3
£4,001 - 4,500   4
£4,501 - 5,000   5
£5,001 - 5,500   6
£5,501 - 6,000   7
£6,001 plus   8

308 ☐

23. When did you finish your full-time education?

> At or below 15 years?
> Between 15 and 20 years?
> After degree or other qualification
>   at a university or a similar place
>   of higher education?

Thank you very much for your co-operation

For Office use only

309

310

311

108